THE
REAL ESTATE
MATH
HANDBOOK

Simplified Solutions for the Real Estate Investor

Jamaine Burrell

THE REAL ESTATE MATH HANDBOOK: SIMPLIFIED SOLUTIONS FOR THE REAL ESTATE INVESTOR

Copyright © 2007 by Atlantic Publishing Group, Inc.
1405 SW 6th Ave. • Ocala, Florida 34471 • 800-814-1132 • 352-622-1875–Fax
Web site: www.atlantic-pub.com • E-mail: sales@atlantic-pub.com
SAN Number: 268-1250

ISBN-13: 978-0-910627-07-8   ISBN-10: 0-910627-07-X

Burrell, Jamaine, 1958-
  The real estate math handbook : simplified solutions for the real estate investor / by Jamaine Burrell.
     p. cm.
  ISBN-13: 978-0-910627-07-8 (alk. paper)
  ISBN-10: 0-910627-07-X (alk. paper)
  1. Real estate investment--Mathematics. 2. Investments--Mathematics. 3. Business mathematics. I. Title.

  HD1382.5.B86 2007
  332.63'2401513--dc22
                                    2007028926

EDITOR: Tracie Kendziora • tkendziora@atlantic-pub.com
INTERIOR DESIGN: Vickie Taylor • vtaylor@atlantic-pub.com   Printed on Recycled Paper
PROOFREADER: Angela Adams • aadams@atlantic-pub.com

Printed in the United States

CONTENTS

FOREWORD

Ken Lee

The Real Estate Math Handbook, which can be used for real estate, finance, and investing, may call on your left brain to apply a bit of old-fashioned sweat equity. But this is not a doctorate-level math book that will enable you to calculate the velocity of your spinning head. This book is quite pragmatic. With the knowledge obtained from all or even part of this book, readers can rest assured they have invested in sound principles and old-fashioned, practical math know-how.

Consumer interest in real estate, finance, and investing continues to grow due in large part to a general level of past success by many consumers and a concern about what lies ahead. For some who played the game with blind aggression, fortunes were created by simply participating in past real estate and stock market gold rushes.

That is all about to change ... again. As newer, tougher markets cast aside blind participants, savvy investors gear up for pending opportunities by embracing a foundation of knowledge. The practiced investor understands that knowledge is an investment that will pay handsomely while carrying little risk. Yet seeking the right knowledge requires care. There is plenty of sound information available, but it is often mixed with instant remedies for our millionaire status shortfall, as hawked by a plethora of gold rush information vendors.

If you are seeking a spiritual swami to give you permission to attract multiple streams of income, a life coach to redefine the meaning of wealth, or an infomercial guru to help flip your investments like hotcakes, you will find one.

But not on planet Earth. Here, maybe all you need or want is a little edge in knowledge, influence, and enlightenment as markets tighten. *The Real Estate Math Handbook* is a well-rounded resource book based on truths, not philosophies – that is math. The book is written in layers and organized well enough to be an accompaniment to a college level course in real estate or investing. It is also a fabulous reference book and an essential tool for one's ongoing journey of financial understanding.

Ken Lee is a top-producing real estate broker in Southern California, real estate investor, and small business coach. He holds a Bachelor of Science degree in Materials Engineering from the University of Pennsylvania and an MBA from Carnegie Mellon University.

Contact Information:
Ken Lee
661-644-3967
Ken@KenLeeHomes.com
www.KenLeeHomes.com

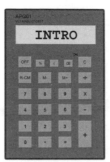

INTRODUCTION

Mathematics is the backbone of progress in our society. We did not just stumble into the age of information technology, and computers are not just a matter of happenstance. Information technology, information science, or however you want to refer to it, is not so much an advance in information as it is an advance in mathematics. The need to perform more complete, more complex, more repetitive, and more precise computations led to the development of computers, and thus, the massive flow of information. Every computer system is based on mathematical computations, numeric and logical. Not to worry, the mathematics presented in this book do not give rise to that level of mathematical computation.

This book presents some of the most fundamental arithmetic, algebraic, and logical concepts used in mathematics. While computers have provided for the solution to many mathematical problems by simply allowing users to input data and then providing a result, this type of problem solving may be detrimental if the user has no understanding of what the data really represents or how the data is used. This book is intended to assist readers in understanding the data used in real estate, finance, and investments.

Chapter One, "Basic Mathematics," gives an overview of the basic mathematical principles. Topics range from basic arithmetic and elementary algebra to basic measurements and elementary statistics. This chapter not only covers the basic mathematical principles used in numerical computations, it also includes an overview of the basic principles of logic and inference. For those readers who have a good grasp on basic mathematics, this chapter simply provides a review of material.

Chapter Two, "Rate of Interest," is devoted to the various methods used in computing interest rates. Both simple interest and compound interest computations are explained. Interest rates, discounts, periodic rates, conversion periods, and other concepts involving interest are explained.

Chapter Three, "Investment Mathematics," discusses the mathematical concepts used in investments and acquiring investment capital. This chapter covers the borrowing, lending, and leveraging of money.

Chapter Four, "Real Estate Mathematics," covers the mathematics used in real estate. It includes real estate measurements, descriptions, types, market valuation, brokers, commission, and depreciation. This chapter also discusses the mathematics of mortgages.

Chapter Five, "Income Property Valuation," deals with the mathematics used in the valuation of income property. It includes computations used to evaluate performance, including cash flows, returns on investment, and various performance ratios.

Chapter Six, "Investment Mathematics," is devoted to the mathematics used in finance. It includes the types of financing and the mathematics of notes, annuities, and bonds.

Chapter Seven, "Technical Analysis," introduces the Excel spreadsheet as a tool to assist in performing various computations.

CHAPTER 1

BASIC MATHEMATICS

Basic mathematics includes an understanding of fundamental arithmetic and algebra. Arithmetic deals with the concepts and operations of numbers, while algebra deals with the concepts and operations of symbols. Knowledge of arithmetic is essential in business, finance, and real estate. However, algebra is not always thought to be essential since many individuals are said to have succeeded in various forms of business and investment with very little knowledge of algebra. The author of this book begs to differ with that assumption. Knowledge of algebra is essential to the success of business, finance, and real estate; however, some successful individuals have relied on others to manage their affairs where such knowledge was required. In businesses and investments of all of sizes and compositions, simple problems will arise that can be readily solved with the application of arithmetic operations and algebraic principles. In many instances, only a fundamental knowledge is necessary. This chapter includes a comprehensive review of basic arithmetic operations and algebraic principles.

Our number system is thought to have derived from the number of fingers on one's hand. The term digit is derived from the Latin term *digitus*, which means hand. The number ten was established as the highest counting number, with additional numbers added to it. Numbers were identified as ten-and-one, ten-and-two, and so forth, which are known today as eleven, twelve, and so forth. Our number system incorporates both a real number system and an imaginary number system. The real number system includes integers, rational numbers, and irrational numbers. Integers include positive and negative whole numbers, such as -3, -2, -1, 0, 1, 2, 3. Rational numbers are any numbers that may be represented as one integer divided by another, such as 1/2, 3/4, 5/8, and so on. Irrational numbers are those numbers for which it is impossible to find any two integers that may be divided to represent it, such as π or $\sqrt{3}$. The imaginary number system is derived from taking the square root of negative numbers and is beyond the scope of this particular book.

The real number system is base ten using the digits 1, 2, 3, 4, 5, 6, 7, 8, 9, and 0. A digit is a single number. The real number system includes principles of position or place value. The value of a number depends on two factors: the particular digits used in stating it and the position of the digits when expressing it. In whole numbers, the rightmost digit indicates the unit digit and the second rightmost digit indicates tens, as shown below. Each digit's position is assigned a value ten times greater than the one preceding it. The most commonly used digit positions are as follows:

quadrillions	hundred trillion	ten trillions	trillions	hundred billions	ten billions	billions	hundred millions	ten millions	millions	hundred thousand	ten thousands	thousands	hundreds	tens	units
8,	3	2	9,	6	9	4,	1	5	2,	8	7	0,	6	1	3

The number shown above is read: 8 quadrillion, 329 trillion, 694 billion, 152 million, 870 thousand, 6 hundred, and 13.

ARITHMETIC

Arithmetic is the study of numbers. The four arithmetic operations, addition, subtraction, multiplication, and division, require an understanding of whole, rational, and irrational numbers. The set of rational and irrational numbers is called decimal numbers. Before the advent of computers and calculators, various methods were developed to simplify and verify arithmetic operations with such numbers. Methods included columnar arithmetic, developing tables, casting out numbers, and the like. Today, one needs only to acquire a low cost calculator to perform such operations.

The four major arithmetic operations may be expressed as follows:

Addition	Addend + Addend = Sum
Subtraction	Minuend – Subtrahend = Difference
Multiplication	Multiplicand * Multiplier = Product
Division	Dividend ÷ Divisor = Quotient

Integer Values

Integers are the set of whole numbers which includes positive numbers and negative numbers, as well as zero. With most positive values, no symbol is used to denote that a value is positive. The positive sign of the value is implied. Most negative values, on the other hand, are denoted with a minus sign, documented in red font, enclosed in parenthesis, or denoted with some combination of the above. When dealing in monetary systems, the sign of a value is of great importance since it determines whether an amount is added or subtracted from another value. It may signify an account debit or a credit, or it may signify whether an amount has been paid or is outstanding. In the arithmetical statement, $8 + 9 = 17$, the implication is $+8 +9 = +17$. Likewise, in the arithmetical statement, $8 - 9 = -1$, the implication is $+8 -9 = -1$.

Factoring

The ability to factor whole numbers and to recognize those factors will assist in the understanding of many arithmetic and algebraic operations, particularly those involving fractions and the reduction of equations, which will be discussed later in this chapter. Factors of whole numbers are the exact divisors of those whole numbers. There are two types of factors: prime factors and composite factors.

Prime factors exist for prime numbers, which are numbers that are exactly divisible by only one and themselves. The prime numbers that are less than 20 include the following: 1, 2, 3, 5, 7, 11, 13, 17, and 19. These numbers are only divisible by one and by themselves. For example, 19 is only divisible by 1 and by 19.

$$\frac{19}{1} = 19$$

$$\frac{19}{19} = 1$$

A composite factor exists for composite numbers, which are numbers that are exactly divisible by numbers other than one and itself. The composite numbers that are less than 20 include the following: 4, 6, 8, 9, 10, 12, 14, 15, 16, and 18. As an example, the number 18 is exactly divisible by 2, 3, 6, and 9 since the following are true:

$$2 * 9 = 18$$
$$2 * 3 * 3 = 18$$
$$6 * 3 = 18$$

Some general rules apply to factors, and they include the following:

- 2 is a factor of any even integer. The numbers 2, 4, 6, 8, 10, 12, and so on have 2 as a factor.

- 5 is a factor of any integer ending in zero or five. The numbers 5, 10, 15, 20, 25, and so on have 5 as a factor.

- 3 is a factor of any integer where the sum of the digits is exactly divisible by three.

Examples:

The number 9 has only a single digit, and it is divisible by 3. As such, 3 is a factor of 9.

The number 18 includes the two digits 1 and 8, which have a sum of 1 + 8 = 9. The sum, 9, is divisible by 3. As such, the number 18 has 3 as a factor since 6 * 3 = 18 and 2 * 3 * 3 = 18.

The number 741 includes the three digits 7, 4, and 1, which have the sum 7 + 4 + 1 = 12. The sum, 12, is divisible by 3. As such, the number 741 has 3 as a factor since 3 * 247 = 741.

- Any integer where the last digit of the integer is the same as the divisor and the other digits, from left to right, are singly exactly divisible or exactly divisible in pairs by the divisor, is itself divisible by the divisor and has the divisor as a factor.

Examples:

The number 8 is a factor of 248 since the last digit of 248 is an 8 and the other digits (from left to right), 24, are also exactly divisible by 8.

The number 7 is a factor of 63,217 since the last digit of 63,217 is a 7 and the other digits, 6321, are exactly divisible by 7, both singly and as the pairs 63 and 21. It is true that 6321 = 7 * 903. It is also true that 63 = 7 * 9 and 21 = 7 * 3.

The process of factoring numbers, like many other mathematical operations, looks more complicated than it really is. Outside practice exercises, one would not normally have to document each step of the process as is done here. The demonstrated steps are usually done in one's head once the process is practiced and understood. With practice and one's elementary education in multiplication and division, it should become intuitive, for example, that 6 and 3 are factors of 18.

Square Root

A square root is a more complicated form of division where the divisor is equal to the quotient. When a value is multiplied by itself, such as 5 * 5 = 25, the value is considered squared. Conversely, a square root defines the squared number. For example, the square root of 25 is 5. The square of any whole number is considered to be a perfect square.

The notation for square root is $^{index}\sqrt{radicand}$. The $\sqrt{}$ symbol is called a radical sign. When no index is specified in the notation, it indicates a square root of the radicand. If a value is specified as the index, it indicates the nth root of the radicand. If, for example, the number 3 is expressed as the index, the third root (or cubic root) is specified. The cubic root of 27, for example, is expressed as $^{3}\sqrt{27}$, since 3 * 3 * 3 = 27.

Absolute Value

Another concept that is used in arithmetic, as well as algebra, is that of an absolute value. The absolute value has application when interpreting directional numbers, such as those used in graphical methods. In most graphical methods, the number of units measured to place a point is determined relative to the origin, which is usually designated as zero. Negative numbers are then positioned in the negative direction (to the left) of the origin. Likewise, positive numbers are positioned in the positive direction (to the right) of the origin. A typical line used in graphical methods is shown below.

The number of units in any given direction is the absolute value of that number. The absolute value is expressed as two vertical bars that enclose a number. The absolute value of 4 is expressed as | 4 | and the absolute value of -4 is expressed as | -4 |. Both expressions are equal to 4.

$$| 4 | = 4$$
$$| -4 | = 4$$

Whether movement is four units from the origin in the positive direction or four units in the negative direction, the absolute number of units moved is four.

Division by Zero

Any real number may be added to, subtracted from, or multiplied by zero, but division by zero is undefined, except when zero is divided by itself. In this case:

$$\frac{0}{0} = 0$$

$$\frac{5}{0} = 0$$

$$\frac{x}{0} = 0$$

For those who choose to automate calculations using spreadsheets or other means of digital computing, exceptions must be incorporated in the development of their chosen algorithms to avoid any division by zero. In the early days of computer programming, division by zero was cause for a variety of errors and failures, as various computer operating systems and software systems handled the division in differing ways. Some systems provided for division by zero to be set to zero; others drew a random number from somewhere in memory. In both instances, the resulting calculations were wrong. Other systems that were designed to recognize the undefined operation created a system crash, often supplemented with appropriate error messages.

Fractions

There are two basic types of fractions: common fractions and improper fractions. Fractions are expressed as follows:

$$\frac{\text{numerator}}{\text{denominator}} = \text{quotient}$$

$$\text{numerator} \div \text{denominator} = \text{quotient}$$

Common fractions are parts of numbers that are represented as the quotient of two whole numbers, such as 1/3 and 1/8. Common fractions are also referred to as proper fractions Proper fractions are fractions in which the numerator is less than the denominator.

An improper fraction is a fraction in which the numerator is greater than the denominator, such as 11/3 or 36/9. An improper fraction may be converted to a mixed number, which is a combination of an integer and a fraction. The improper fraction 11/3 is converted to a mixed number by performing the implied division as follows:

$$\frac{11}{3} = 3\frac{2}{3}$$

Fractions with differing denominators cannot be added or subtracted unless they are converted to fractions with a common denominator. In such instances, the least common denominator (LCD) should be sought. The LCD is the lowest number for which all the denominators are factors. The LCD may be found by expressing each denominator in terms of its prime factors. As an example, the fractions 4/5, 5/12, 6/15, 1/18, and 7/24 are to be added. The prime factors of each of the denominators is as follows:

$$5 \quad = 1 * 5$$
$$12 \quad = 2 * 2 * 3$$
$$15 \quad = 5 * 3$$
$$18 \quad = 2 * 3 * 3$$
$$24 \quad = 2 * 2 * 2 * 3$$

The lowest common multiple of the denominators must now be found. This implies finding the prime factors that are expressed the greatest number of times. In our example:

- 1 is expressed only once as a factor of 5.

- 2 is expressed once as a factor of 18, twice as a factor of 12, and three times as a factor of 24.

   ᵒ As such, 2 is expressed the most number of times as a factor of 24.

- 3 is expressed once as a factor of 24, 15, and 12, and twice as a factor of 18.

   ᵒ As such, 3 is expressed the most number of times as a factor of 18.

- 5 is expressed only once as a factor of 5 and 15.

   So, 1 (1's), 3 (2's), 2 (3's) and 1 (5's) = 1 * 2 * 2 * 2 * 3 * 3 * 5 = 360.

   ᵒ Thus, the LCD is 360.

This process of factoring prime numbers is another process that looks more complicated than it really is. Again, with practice and knowledge of multiplication and division, the process of factoring a value becomes intuitive.

Common Denominators

A common denominator may always be found by multiplying all the denominators together, but this may not result in the LCD. The operative word is "least." A common denominator for 2/6 and 3/9 may be found by multiplying the denominators, 6 * 9 = 54. Though 54 is a common denominator, it is not the LCD. The prime factors of the denominators provide the LCD. The prime factors of 6 and 9 are as follows:

$$6 = 2 * 3$$
$$9 = 3 * 3$$

Since 1 (2's) and 2 (3's) implies 2 * 3 * 3 = 18, the LCD is 18.

The ability to determine the common denominator of fractional numbers is also necessary for comparing fractional numbers. One may find it difficult to determine if 7/16 is greater than 5/12 until both fractions are expressed with a common denominator. When both fractions share a common denominator, the numerators may then be used to determine which fractional number is greater. As an example, the values 7/16 and 5/12 have a LCD of 48, such that

$$\frac{7}{16} = \frac{21}{48}$$
$$\frac{5}{12} = \frac{20}{48}$$

It is clear from the conversion that 7/16 is greater than 5/12 since 21 is greater than 20.

Rules for Addition and Subtraction of Fractions

The addition and subtraction of common fractions should follow these simple rules:

- Express the fractions with a common denominator, preferably the LCD.

- Add or subtract the numerators.

- Convert the resulting sum or difference to lowest terms.

Example:

$$\frac{2}{3} - \frac{1}{4}$$

$$= \frac{8}{12} - \frac{3}{12}$$

$$= \frac{8-3}{12}$$

$$= \frac{5}{12}$$

Addition and Subtraction of Mixed Number Fractions

Rules for the addition and subtraction of mixed number fractions are as follows:

- Add or subtract the integer portions of the mixed numbers.

- Add or subtract the fractional portions of the mixed numbers following the rules outlined above.

- Combine the sums or differences.

- In subtraction, if the minuend is less than the subtrahend, 1 must be subtracted from the integer part of the minuend and added to the fractional part of the minuend to form a new, yet equal, statement.

Example:

In the statement 27 – 22(11/16), 27 is an integer with fractional part = 0/0. As such, the fractional part of the minuend is 0 and the fractional part of the subtrahend is 11/16. Since there is no fractional part of the minuend, one must be taken from the integer part of the minuend and added to the fractional part as follows:

$$27 \ = \ 27 \, \frac{0}{0} \ = \ 26 \, \frac{16}{16}$$

A new statement is formed and solved as follows:

$$27 \ - \ 22 \, \frac{11}{16}$$

$$= \ 26 \, \frac{16}{16} \ - \ 22 \, \frac{11}{16}$$

$$= \ 26 \ - \ 22 \ + \ \frac{16}{16} \ - \ \frac{11}{16}$$

$$= \ 4 \ + \ \frac{5}{16}$$

$$= \ 4 \, \frac{5}{16}$$

Rules for Multiplication of Fractions

Multiplication involving common fractions may include multiplying an integer by a fraction (or vice versa) or multiplying a fraction by a fraction. In the multiplication of an integer by a fraction, or vice versa, the integer value should be converted into a fraction before completing the operation. After the fractional numbers are expressed, the numerators should be multiplied together and the denominators should be multiplied together to form a new fraction. The new fraction should then be reduced to the lowest terms.

Example:

The product of 5 * 3/4 is solved by first converting the integer into a fraction as follows:

$$5 = 5/1$$

A new statement is then formed and solved as follows:

$$\frac{5}{1} * \frac{3}{4}$$

$$= \frac{5 * 3}{1 * 4}$$

$$= \frac{15}{4}$$

$$= 3 \frac{3}{4}$$

In the multiplication of common fractions, factors common to both the numerators and denominators may be sought to create cancellation and simplify the multiplication process. Numerators and denominators should be reduced to prime factors to create candidates for cancellation as follows:

$$\frac{7}{12} * \frac{9}{16} * \frac{4}{21}$$

$$= \frac{7 * 9 * 4}{12 * 16 * 21}$$

$$= \frac{\cancel{7} * 1 * \cancel{3} * \cancel{3} * \cancel{2} * \cancel{2}}{\cancel{3} * \cancel{2} * \cancel{2} * 2 * 2 * 2 * 2 * \cancel{7} * \cancel{3}}$$

$$= \frac{1}{2 * 2 * 2 * 2}$$

$$= \frac{1}{16}$$

Multiplication of Mixed Number Fractions

Rules for the multiplication of fractions when one of the fractions is a mixed number may be accomplished by one of two methods.

Method 1:

- Convert the mixed numbers to improper fractions.

- Multiply the resulting fractions.

Example 1:

The product of 48(1/2) * 3(2/3) is found as follows:

Convert the mixed numbers to improper fractions:

$$48(1/2) = 97/2 \text{ and } 3(2/3) = 11/3$$

So,

$$\frac{97}{2} * \frac{11}{3}$$

$$= \frac{97 * 11}{2 * 3}$$

$$= \frac{1067}{6}$$

$$= 177 \frac{5}{6}$$

Method 2:

- Multiply the integer part of the first value by the integer part of the second value, if one exists.

- Multiply the integer part of the first value by the fractional part of the second value, if it exists.

- Multiply the fractional part of the first value by the integer part of the second value, if it exists.

- Multiply the fractional part of the first value by the fractional part of the second value, if it exists.

- Add the partial products.

Example 2:

Using the same example as above, 48(1/2) * 3(2/3), the product is found as follows:

$$48 \quad * \quad 3 \quad + \quad 48 \, \frac{2}{3} \quad + \quad 3 \, \frac{1}{2} \quad + \quad \frac{1}{2} \, * \, \frac{2}{3}$$

$$= \quad 144 \quad + \quad 32 \quad + \quad \frac{3}{2} \quad + \quad \frac{2}{6}$$

The rules for addition of mixed number fractions is used to find the sum of the partial products. Since 6 is the LCD of the fractional partial products, the sum becomes:

$$144 \quad + \quad 32 \quad + \quad \frac{9}{6} \quad + \quad \frac{2}{6}$$

$$= \quad 176 \quad + \quad \frac{9 \, + \, 2}{6}$$

$$= \quad 176 \quad + \quad \frac{11}{6}$$

$$= \quad 176 \quad + \quad 1 \, \frac{5}{6}$$

$$= \quad 177 \, \frac{5}{6}$$

Rules for Division of Fractions

In the multiplication of common fractions, it is understood that

$$8 \quad * \quad \frac{1}{2}$$

$$= \quad \frac{8 \, * \, 1}{1 \, * \, 2}$$

$$= \quad \frac{8}{2}$$

$$= \quad 4$$

The fraction 1/2 is the reciprocal of 2. The reciprocal of a number is 1 divided by that number. As such, the product of a number and its reciprocal is always equal to one. The product of 8 and its reciprocal is one.

$$\cancel{8} \quad * \quad \frac{1}{\cancel{8}} \quad = \quad 1$$

In division, the quotient obtained by dividing one number by another is equivalent to multiplying the numerator by the reciprocal of the denominator.

Example 1:

$$\frac{8}{2}$$

$$= 8 \quad * \quad \frac{1}{2}$$

$$= \frac{8 \quad * \quad 1}{1 \quad * \quad 2}$$

$$= 4$$

If the numerator and denominator of a fraction are interchanged, a reciprocal is formed. This interchange of terms is known as inverting a fraction. The product of multiplying a fraction by its reciprocal is always equal to one. The reciprocal of $^2/_8$ is $^8/_2$. The product $^2/_8 * ^8/_2 = ^{16}/_{16} = 1$.

The division of common fractions makes use of this method of reciprocals such that the division of common fractions involves multiplication. Division involving common fractions may include dividing an integer by a fraction (or vice versa) or dividing a fraction by a fraction. In the division of an integer by a fraction, or vice versa, the fraction should be multiplied by the reciprocal of the integer before completing the operation. The new fraction should then be reduced to the lowest terms.

Example 2:

The quotient $^3/_4 \div 5$ is solved by first converting the integer into its reciprocal as follows:

The reciprocal of 5 is $^1/_5$.

A new statement is then formed and solved as follows:

$$\frac{3}{4} \, * \, \frac{1}{5}$$

$$= \frac{3 \, * \, 1}{4 \, * \, 5}$$

$$= \frac{3}{20}$$

In the division of two fractions, the divisor must be inverted to create a multiplication operation. Inverting the divisor has the effect of creating a multiplication operation in which the dividend is multiplied by the reciprocal of the divisor.

Example 3:

The quotient of $^5/_6 \div ^4/_5$ is solved as follows:

$$\frac{\frac{5}{6}}{\frac{4}{5}}$$

$$= \frac{5}{6} \, * \, \frac{5}{4}$$

$$= \frac{5 \, * \, 5}{6 \, * \, 4}$$

$$= \frac{25}{24}$$

$$= 1 \, \frac{1}{24}$$

Division of Mixed Number Fractions

To divide fractions when one of the fractions is a mixed number, the mixed number is converted into an improper fraction and the rules for the division of common fractions are followed.

Example:

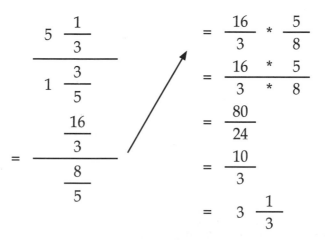

$$\frac{5\frac{1}{3}}{1\frac{3}{5}} = \frac{\frac{16}{3}}{\frac{8}{5}}$$

$$= \frac{16}{3} * \frac{5}{8}$$

$$= \frac{16 * 5}{3 * 8}$$

$$= \frac{80}{24}$$

$$= \frac{10}{3}$$

$$= 3\frac{1}{3}$$

Division is the process of determining how many times one number is contained in another. If the divisor is not a factor of the dividend, the result of the division process includes a remainder. This remainder may be expressed as either a fraction of the dividend or a decimal value.

Decimals

Most calculations in business, investment, and real estate are not as reliant on integers or fractions as they are on decimal values. Integers are seldom used because integers provide poor units of measure. Integers, for example, cannot provide the precision necessary to determine whether a measured distance is 4 feet or 4.5 feet. Fractions are seldom used because fractional numbers, particularly those with large numerators or denominators, can be awkward and are best understood when converted to decimal form. A measurement is more likely to be presented as 0.0255 rather than 5/196. Prices are stated in dollar and cents, which are decimal values. Decimal values include amounts that are less than a single unit (or 1), such a fifty cents ($0.50).

When a fraction is converted to decimal form, it is considered a pure decimal. When a mixed number is converted to decimal form, it is considered a mixed decimal. The addition, subtraction, multiplication, and division of decimal numbers are carried out similarly to that of whole numbers. Care must be taken, however, to properly place the decimal point.

Decimal numbers may be presented with differing levels of accuracy so that results from one calculation may differ somewhat from other calculations, though they are in actuality the same. When accuracy is specified to a certain number of significant digits, this means that all the digits may be read directly, except the last digit. The last digit is an interpolation or rounding. In most businesses and other activities that involve money, the precision of decimal numbers is usually limited to two decimal places beyond the decimal point.

Interpolation

Interpolation is a method for estimating a value when values greater than and less than an unknown value are known. Interpolation involves proportions. The proportional units between known values must first be determined, and the interpolated value is then computed within those same proportions. It is important to remember that an interpolated value is not exact, but an estimate or approximation.

Example:

The return on five investment accounts is released every two weeks as follows:

	Account A	Account B	Account C	Account D	Account F
Week 2	16.3%	18.5%	19.5%	17.5%	16.9%
Week 4	15.8%	16.7%	17.4%	17.2%	15.9%
Week 6	15.7%	15.5%	15.0%	16.2%	15.4%
Week 8	12.4%	13.2%	14.2%	15.1%	15.3%

Between weeks 4 and 6, Account D decreased from 17.2% to 16.2%. We want to estimate the return at week 5. From the data, we know that, between weeks 4 and 6, the difference was 1%.

2	1	Week 4	17.2%	x%	1%
		Week 5			
		Week 6	16.2%		

The time difference between week 4 and week 5 is 1 and between week 4 and week 6 it is 2. The difference in returns between week 4 and week 5 is what we are attempting to define and the difference between week 4 and week 6 is 1%. The proportion is as follows:

$$\frac{1 \text{ wks}}{2 \text{ wks}} = \frac{x\%}{1\%}$$

$$x\% = 1\% * \frac{1 \, \cancel{\text{wks}}}{2 \, \cancel{\text{wks}}}$$

$$= 1 * \frac{1}{2}$$

$$= \frac{1}{2}$$

$$= 0.5\%$$

Since x = 0.5%, we may either subtract 0.5% from the return for week 4 or add 0.5% to the return for week 6 to arrive at the estimated return for week 5. At week 5, the return is estimated to be:

$$17.2\% - 0.5\%$$
$$= 16.7\%$$

$$\text{or}$$
$$16.2\% + 0.5\%$$
$$= 16.7\%$$

The estimated return for week 5 is 16.7%.

Decimal Multiplication

In the multiplication of two decimal values, the resulting product should include the placement of the decimal point as many places to the right as there are places in the multiplicand and multiplier. In the product 38.274 * 5.43 = 207.82782, the total number of decimal places is 3 (in the multiplicand) + 2 (in the multiplier) = 5.

When multiplying a decimal value by a value that is a power of 10, such as 100 (100 = 10^2), the decimal point of the decimal value must be moved as many places to the right as there are zeros in the value that is a power of 10.

$$2.4586 * 10 = 24.586$$
$$2.4586 * 100 = 245.86$$
$$2.4586 * 1000 = 2458.6$$
$$2.4586 * 10,000 = 24,586$$
$$2.4586 * 100,000 = 245,860$$
$$2.4586 * 10,000,000 = 2,458,600$$

In the product of two decimal values, the decimal point may be moved the same number of places, in opposite directions, without affecting the proper calculation of the product.

Example:

The product: 18.62 * 3.8 = 70.8
and so too is the product: 186.2 * 0.38 = 70.8
and the product: 1.862 * 38 = 70.8

Decimal Division

In the division of two decimal values, the decimal point of either the divisor or dividend may be moved the same number of places, in the same direction, without affecting the proper calculation of the quotient.

Example:

The quotient: $18.62 \div 3.8 = 4.9$
and so too is the quotient: $186.2 \div 38 = 4.9$
and the quotient: $1.862 \div .38 = 4.9$

Locating the decimal point in the quotient of decimal division is fundamental. If the divisor is a whole number, the decimal point should be placed as many places to the right as there are places in the dividend. If the divisor is not a whole number, the decimal point of the divisor should be moved to the right of the last digit in the divisor, and the decimal point of the dividend should be moved an equal number of places to the right. This has the effect of converting the divisor to a whole number. If the dividend does not have enough digits to accommodate the decimal placement, zeros should be added. The decimal point of the quotient is then placed as many places to the right as there are places in the dividend.

Significant Digits

Whole numbers are exact numbers, whereas decimal and fractional numbers are approximated values. No measurement or decimal value is absolutely correct. These types of approximated values are known to be correct only to some number of significant digits.

The number zero has particular importance as a significant digit. Zeros are significant digits if they occur between two nonzero digits or if the zero is the final digit to the right of a decimal point. As examples, the values 130.08 and 130.80 have 5 significant digits. A zero used to locate a decimal point is not significant. For example, the values 0.08 and 0.8 have only one significant digit.

Values have the same precision if they are given the same number of decimal places. The value 0.08 has the same precision as the value 130.08, which has 5 significant digits. The significance of a digit is dependent on the application for which it is being used. The value 2,500 may have two, three, or four significant digits if it is used as a measure of distance, but if it is used as a count of money ($2,500) it has four significant digits. Two rules apply to significant digits as follows:

- In multiplication and division, the number of significant digits in a product or quotient is the same as that in the least significant of the values used to calculate the product or quotient. As an example, the product 16 * 35.6 = 569.6, has only two significant digits since 16 is the least significant of the values used in forming the product. The product should be written 16 * 35.6 = 57. However, if it were predetermined that 16 was an integer good for an infinite number of decimal places, the product would have three significant figures based on the value 35.6. The product would be correctly written as 16 * 35.6 = 570.

- In addition and subtraction, the number of significant digits is the same as that of the least accurate value used in the calculation.

Percentages

The principles of fractions and decimals have application in real estate and other disciplines that deal with percentages. When two things are compared with one another, that comparison is oftentimes expressed as a percentage. Percent is expressed by the symbol % and is synonymous with the concept of rate.

Percentages provide another way of expressing fractional or decimal values. The percent symbol is merely a substitute for the decimal point in a decimal value or the quantity, 100, in the denominator of a fraction. As such, 75% = 0.75 = 75/100. To express a fraction as a percent, the fraction must first be converted to a decimal value by performing the required division. After the division is performed, the decimal point is moved two places to the right and the % symbol is affixed as follows:

$$7 \div 15 = 0.4666... = 46.6...\% = 46.6\%$$

The precision used in dealing with percentages is dependent upon the individual or system making use of the values. In monetary systems, precision to one or two decimal places is usually sufficient.

To convert a percent to a fraction, the % symbol must be removed and one of the following procedures must be followed. Allow the percentage to become the numerator of the fraction with a denominator of 100 or, if the percentage is expressed as a fraction, multiply the denominator by 100. Then, reduce the newly acquired fraction to its lowest terms.

Example 1:

$$46.6\% \quad \frac{46.6}{100} = \frac{23.3}{50}$$

Example 2:

$$\frac{2}{3}\% = \frac{2}{3 * 100} = \frac{2}{300} = \frac{1}{150}$$

There are three basic types of percentage calculations, which include finding the percentage rate, finding the percent of a number, and finding the base number when the percentage is known.

Finding the Percentage Rate

Finding the percentage rate involves finding what percent one number is of another. As an example, one may need to answer the query, 20 is what percent of 60? In other words, 20 are how many hundredths of 60? The query is answered as follows:

$$20 \div 60 = 0.333\ldots$$
rounding to 2 decimal places,
$$0.333\ldots = 0.33 = 33\%$$

Finding the Percent of a Number

Finding the percent of a number equates to the multiplication of two numbers, the base number and the percentage rate. In the query, what is 20% of 60, 20% is the percentage rate and 60 is the base number. The query is answered as follows:

$$20\% * 60 = .20 * 60 = 12.0 = 12\%$$

Finding the Base Number

Finding the base number when the percentage and percentage rate are known involves a division operation. The percentage is divided by the percentage rate. In the query, 20 is 60% of what number, 20 is percentage and 60% is the percentage rate. The query is answered as follows:

$$\frac{20}{60\%} = \frac{20}{.60} = 33.3\ldots = 33.3$$

Common Fractional Equivalents

Fractional equivalents are used to simplify the mathematics of fractions. Some fraction equivalents are used more often in science and business than others. Some commonly used fractional equivalents are shown in Table 1.

Table 1: Common Fractional Equivalents					
Fraction	Percent	Fraction	Percent	Fraction	Percent
1/8	= 12(1/2)%	1/25	= 4%	7/8	= 87(1/2)%
1/6	= 16(2/3)%	1/24	= 4(1/6)%	2/3	= 66(2/3)%
1/5	= 20%	1/18	= 5(5/9)%	3/4	= 75%
1/4	= 25%	1/16	= 6(1/4)%	5/6	= 83(1/3)%
1/3	= 33(1/3)%	1/15	= 6(2/3)%	5/12	= 41(2/3)%
1/2	= 50%	1/12	= 8(1/3)%	7/12	= 58(1/3)%
1/75	= 1(1/3)%	1/9	= 11(1/9)%	5/16	= 31(1/4)%
1/40	= 2(1/2)%	3/8	= 37(1/2)%	9/16	= 56(1/4)%
1/30	= 3(1/3)%	5/8	= 62(1/2)%		

Aliquant Parts

An aliquant part is a fractional part. The equivalents shown in Table 1 are aliquant parts of 100%. If an aliquant part is known, any other aliquant part can be found by multiplying the initial aliquant part by the numerator of the new aliquant part. As an example:

$$\text{If it is known that } 16(^2/_3)\% = \text{ }^1/_6 \text{ of } 100\%$$
$$\text{then } ^3/_6 \text{ of } 100\% \text{ is calculated as follows:}$$
$$3 * 16(^2/_3)\%$$
$$= 48(^6/_3)\% = 50\%$$

As another example: $^5/_{24}$ of 100% is calculated as follows:

$$(^5/_{24}) = 5(^1/_{24})$$
$$\text{from Table 1, } ^1/_{24} \text{ is } 4(^1/_6)\% \text{ of } 100\%$$
$$\text{then}$$
$$5 * 4(^1/_6)\%$$
$$= 20(^5/_6)\%$$

ELEMENTARY ALGEBRA

One of the first requisites for finding solutions to problems is the ability to express relationships in algebraic symbols. To be able to express such relationships, an understanding of the most elementary arithmetic and algebraic relationships and their significance is necessary. Various types of algebraic relationships are used in business, finance, and real estate to solve problems involving relationships between variables, percentages, proportions, discounts, rates of return, and so on.

Literals

In arithmetic, operations are performed on Arabic numbers. In algebra, letters of the alphabet replace Arabic numbers. These letters may have different numerical values assigned to them. These letters are called literal numbers or literals. Literal numbers are symbols used in algebra to represent numbers and to perform operations on those numbers. Literals make it easier to state mathematical definitions in a generalized form. The literal statement, a > b signifies that, on a number scale, the value represented by a is greater than the value represented by b. In algebra, when a literal symbol is used to represent a value that may vary, the literal symbol is known as a variable. If the literal symbol is used to represent the same value throughout a discussion or problem, the literal symbol is called a constant.

Algebraic Terms

Literal numbers, such as a, b, and c, as well as products such as 2a and 3bx, are called algebraic terms. Since 2a represents a product of 2 and a, both 2 and a are factors of 2a. These factors are called coefficients of the algebraic term. Since 2 is an Arabic numeral, it is considered a numerical coefficient of a. Since a is a literal, it is considered a literal coefficient of 2. Algebraic terms with the same literal coefficient are called like or similar terms. The algebraic terms,

4a and 24a, are considered like terms. Like terms can be added together or subtracted from one another. Unlike terms cannot.

$$4a + 6a - 2a = 8a$$
$$4a + 6b - 2a = 2a - 6b$$

Equations

When algebraic terms are combined with mathematical operators such as +, -, or >, the combination is called an algebraic expression or algebraic statement. An algebraic expression of one term is called a monomial. An algebraic statement of two terms is called a binomial. An algebraic statement of two or more terms is called a polynomial.

Monomial:	$2x$
Binomial:	$2x + 3y$
Polynomial:	$2x + 3y + 4z$

The algebraic statement of $x + x = 2x$ holds true for all values assigned to x. The value of the letter x is considered to be variable. Such equality between two expressions is known as an equation. An equation that holds true for all values of a variable is called an identical equation. An equation that is true for only a certain value or an equation that is true for a specific set of values is called a conditional equation. The values are called unknowns. Any value that is substituted for the unknown in an equation reduces both sides of the equation to the same value. The substituted value is known as the root of the equation and is said to satisfy the equation. To solve an equation is to find the root of the equation that reduces both sides of the equation to the same value.

Axioms of the equality of equations are as follows:

If equals are added to equals, the sums are equal.	If $a+b=x$, then $a+b+c=x+c$
If equals are subtracted from equals, the differences are equal.	If $a+b=x$, then $a+b-c=x-c$

If equals multiply equals, the products are equal.	If $a \div b = x$, then $(a \div b)c = xc$
If equals divide equals, the quotients are equal.	If $a \div b = x$, then $(a \div b) \div c = x \div c$

Equations also follow the rule of transposition, which dictates that any term of an equation may be moved from one side of the equation to the other as long as the algebraic sign of the term is changed. The following equations are equal:

$$a + b = c - d$$
$$\text{and}$$
$$a + d = c - b$$

Monomials and Polynomials

To multiply two monomials, the product of the numerical coefficients and the product of the literal coefficients must be found. If the literal coefficients are the same, the exponent of their product is the sum of the exponents of the coefficients. Only like literal coefficients may be combined. As an example, the monomials $5x^2$ and $4x$ are to be multiplied. The process is as follows:

The numerical coefficients are multiplied: $5 * 4 = 20$
The literal coefficients that are the same are multiplied:
$$x^2 * x = x^{(2+1)} = x^3$$
$$\text{Therefore}$$
$$5x^2 * 4x = 20x^3$$

The product of a monomial and a polynomial is found by multiplying each term of the polynomial by the monomial as follows:

$$3ab\,(5ab^2 + 8a^2b - 4)$$
$$= 15a^2b^3 + 24a^3b^2 - 12ab$$

The product of two binomials is found by multiplying each term of one quantity by each term of the other and adding the results as follows:

$$(3x + 4y) * (3x - 4y)$$
$$= 3x * 3x + 3x * (-4y) + 4y * 3x + 4y * (-4y)$$
$$= 9x^2 - 12xy + 12xy - 16y^2$$
$$= 9x^2 - 16 y^2$$

This particular problem represents a common algebraic relationship: the product of the sum and difference of two numbers. This product is always equal to the square of the first number minus the square of the second number.

$$(x + y) * (x - y)$$
$$= x^2 - y^2$$

Another commonly used relationship is the multiplication of a sum or difference by itself. This product is called a perfect square. The products always take on the following common forms:

$(x + y)^2$	$(x - y)^2$
$= (x + y) * (x + y)$	$= (x - y) * (x - y)$
$= x^2 + 2xy + y^2$	$= x^2 - 2xy + y^2$

Factoring

The process of factoring involves determining the factors that are common to an algebraic expression. When examining equations to factor, the first objective is seeking common forms of equations. Some common products are specified above. In examining an equation, such as $9x^2 + 6x + 1$, a perfect square is recognized since the middle term is equal to twice the product of the square root of the first and third terms, i.e., $9 = 32$, $1 = 12$, and $6 = 2 (3 * 1)$. The statement represents the square of $x + 1$.

$$9x^2 + 6x + 1$$
$$= (3x + 1)^2$$

Another common algebraic relationship specifies that if every term of an algebraic expression contains a common factor, that factor may be removed to create a new expression. In the expression ax = ay, a is common to both terms of the expression, and the expression takes on the following form:

$$ax + ay = a(x + y)$$

In examining the expression, $5x^2 + 10x^2y - 20x^2y^3$, it is apparent that both 5 and x^2 are factors of each term of the equation, and the factor $5x^2$ may be factored out to create a new expression as follows:

$$5x^2 + 10x^2y - 20x^2y^3$$
$$= 5x^2(1 + 2y - 4y^3)$$

Solving Equations

In solving algebraic equations, words and expressions have the same meaning as they do in arithmetic. The sum of 6 and 9 may be stated algebraically as 6 + 9. Likewise, the sum of x and y may be stated as x + y. Certain ideas may be expressed easily with an algebraic equivalent. Some common equivalents are as follows:

Three more than x	x + 3
x increased by 3	x + 3
The sum of x and 3	x + 3
Three greater than x	x + 3
Three less than x	x − 3
The excess of x over 3	x − 3
x reduced by 3	x − 3
Three more than twice x	3 + 2x
3 more than one-half of x	½x + 3
3 less than twice the product of x and y	2xy − 3
The sum of x and y	x + y

The sum of x and y, squared	$(x + y)^2$
The sum of squares of x and y	$x^2 + y^2$
The value of x in pennies	$0.01x$
The value of x apples at y cents per apple	$0.01xy$
The value of x bags of apples at \$2 per bag	$\$2x$

After an appropriate algebraic equation is defined, the equation must then be solved. In business, if a problem occurs frequently with variation only in the numbers used, the most time saving method of solving the problem is to develop a chart of possible solutions. The method may be used by anyone whether or not they understand how the computations for the chart were derived. Charts showing sales taxes, income taxes, logarithms, and other data unique to a need have been developed for use. This method of charting data precludes that all possible solutions are accounted for. Usually this is not the case. A better alternative method for solving these problems involves developing an equation that properly defines the problem and allows one to calculate solutions.

Equations Versus Formulas

A formula is any statement of principle or rule involving magnitudes, expressed in the form of an equation. A formula may be solved for any given unknown; however, formulas often contain operations that cannot be fully carried out. When no particular value is assigned to unknown quantities, a formula cannot be solved.

The relationship between the base (B), rate (R), and percent (P) in percent problems may be stated algebraically as the formula, BR = P. This formula may be easily solved for any of the three unknowns as follows:

$$B = \frac{R}{P} \qquad R = \frac{P}{B} \qquad P = BR$$

An amount A is defined by the relationship A = B + P. The formula for A could then be devised as follows:

$$A = B + P$$
$$\text{Since } P = BR, \text{ then}$$
$$A = B + BR$$
$$A = B\,(1 + R)$$
$$\text{and,}$$

$$B = \frac{A}{1+R}$$

Though a valid formula is established, the mathematical operations cannot be carried out until values are assigned to the unknown variables of the formula.

Laws of Algebra

The fundamental laws of algebra include the cumulative, associative, and distributive laws. The commutative law applies to addition and multiplication. This laws dictates that it does not matter in which order two numbers are added or multiplied; the respective sum or product is the same. As such, 4 + 6 = 10 and 6 + 4 = 10. Likewise, 4 * 6 = 24 and 6 * 4 = 24. The associative law also applies to addition and multiplication. The associative law dictates that the sum or product of three or more numbers is the same regardless of how the numbers are grouped. As such, 2 + (4 + 6) = 12 and (2 + 4) + 6 = 12. Likewise, 2 * (4 * 6) = 48 and (2 * 4) * 6 = 48. The distributive law dictates that the product of one number and the sum of two or more other numbers is equal to the products of the number and each of the numbers of the sum. As such, 4 (3 + 5) = 4 * 3 + 4 * 5. The following literal statements are used to express the fundamental laws of algebra:

Commutative law of addition:	a + b = b + a
Commutative law of multiplication:	ab = ba
Associative law of addition	a + (b + c) = (a + b) + c

| Associative law of multiplication | $a(bc) = (ab)c$ |
| Distributive law | $a(b + c) = ab + ac$ |

Laws of Signs

The laws of signs apply to all real numbers: integers, rational numbers, and irrational numbers, and govern the operations of addition, subtraction, multiplication, and division. The laws of signs are as follows:

Add two real numbers with like signs	Add their absolute values and affix the common sign.
Add two real numbers with unlike signs	Subtract the absolute value of the smaller value from the absolute value of the larger value and affix the sign of the number with the larger absolute value.
Subtract two real numbers	Change the sign of the number to be subtracted, add their absolute values, and affix the sign of the number with the larger absolute value.
Multiply or divide two real numbers with like signs	Calculate the product or quotient of their absolute values.
Multiply or divide two real numbers with unlike signs	Calculate the negative of the product or quotient of their absolute values.

Exponents

In multiplication, it is often times necessary to multiply a number by itself several times. Rather than actually expressing this redundant operation, the notation a^n is used, where a is the base number and n is the exponent that represents the number of times that "a" appears in a product. The expression is termed the nth power of a. The fifth power of 3 is represented as follows:

$$3^5 = 3 * 3 * 3 * 3 * 3 = 243$$

Certain operations with exponents are of particular importance. They include the following:

$a^0 = 0$	
$a^1 = a$	
$a^n * a^m = a^{n+m}$	$a^3 * a^5 = a^{3+5} = a^8$
$a^n \div a^m = a^{n-m}$, $m > 0$ and $a \neq 0$	$a^3 \div a^5 = a^{3-5} = a^{-2}$
$a^n \div a^m = 1 \div a^{m-n}$, $m > 0$ and $a \neq 0$	$a^3 \div a^5 = 1 \div a^{5-3} = 1 \div a^2$
$(a^n)^m = a^{nm}$	$(a^3)^5 = a^{3*5} = a^{15}$
$(ab)^n = a^n b^n$	$(ab)^3 = a^3 b^3$
$(a \div b)^n = a^n \div b^n$, $b \neq 0$	$(a \div b)^3 = a^3 \div b^3$

Extracting a Root

When the process of squaring a number is reversed, the process is called extracting the square root. When a value is squared, as in x^2, the value of x can be found by taking the square root of x^2:

$$\sqrt{x^2} = x$$

The notation $\sqrt{}$ indicates that the value of x may be either a positive or negative value. The arithmetic process to extract the square root of a number involves separating the number into groups of two digits, starting at the decimal point. The number of two digit groups defines the number of digits in the square root. If a number less than ten is squared, there will be only two digits to the left of the decimal point. If the number is more than ten, but less than 100, there will be two sets of two digit numbers to the left of the decimal point. The rest of the process to manually extract a square root is cumbersome and will not be detailed here. A scientific calculator provides the best method of calculating square. The partial process outlined above may be used in assessing the correctness of any digitally computed square root.

In finding the root of an exponential number, the root must divide the exponent. Since any number, a, is presumed to have an exponent of 1 ($a = a^1$), the square root of a is:

$$\sqrt{a} = a^{1/2}$$

Likewise,

$$\sqrt[n]{a} = a^{1/n}$$

and

$$\sqrt[n]{a^m} = a^{m/n}$$

When the index (n) is greater than two, the process of extracting the roots requires the use of logarithms. The process of extracting roots using logarithms is known as evolution. Evolution involves dividing the logarithm of the number by the index of the root and then finding the antilogarithm of the quotient. The manual use of logarithms and antilogarithms in arithmetic processes is too detailed and cumbersome to present here. Such operations are more easily and accurately carried out with some method of digital computation, such as with the use of a scientific calculator or computer software.

Logarithms

A logarithm is the converse of an exponent in the same sense that addition is the converse of subtraction. A logarithm, also called the log of a number, is the exponent of a value expressed as a^n, where a is the base number and n is the exponent. The base may be any number, but a base of 10 is of particular importance since the logarithm of any number to base 10 can be computed using methods of computing the logarithm of numbers between 1 and 10. As such, the logarithm is the exponent to which the number 10 must be raised to express a number. The power of 10 in the expression 10^3 is 3, and 3 is a logarithm. For any value of the form 10^x, the logarithm of 10 is x. This is expressed:

$$\log 10^x = x$$

Before the days of digital computing, individuals performed mathematical operations by hand and used charts and tables to document the results of the more complex and repetitive operations. In the calculation of logarithms, an apparatus known as a slide rule was used, along with tables of logarithms. Tables of logarithms are used to calculate the log of any decimal value. Since it was not practical or possible to create a table of logarithms for every single decimal value, tables were devised to provide solutions for every integer and the mantissa of every decimal value. This book will not provide a discussion of the use of slide rules or tables of logarithms since their use is outdated. However, specific properties of logarithms, including the characteristic and mantissa, will be introduced. It should be noted that tables of logarithms are available for use in the absence of digital computing methods.

Scientific Notation and Standard Position

A number is expressed in standard notation, also called scientific notation, when that number can be expressed as the product of a number between 1 and 10 and a power of 10. Since any decimal number can be expressed as the product of a number between 1 and 10 and a power of 10, any decimal number can be written in scientific notation. Any number expressed in scientific notation can also be expressed in what is called standard position. Standard position is a decimal expression where the decimal point immediately follows the first digit on the left. The decimal value 234.56 is expressed in standard position as $2.3456 * 10^2$.

To express any number in scientific notation, move the decimal point to the standard position and multiply the resulting number by a power of 10. The exponent of 10 will be equal to the number of places the decimal point was shifted. If the decimal point is moved to the left, the exponent will be positive. If the decimal point is moved to the right, the exponent will be negative. As an example, the value .0029487 is expressed in scientific notation as $2.9487 * 10^{-3}$. When numbers are expressed in scientific notation, the same series of digits appear in the expressions. The numbers only differ in the power of 10 used.

The decimal point is understood to exist at the far right of any integer value. As such, the value 56 is understood to be 56., but the decimal point is not usually written. When converting a number to scientific notation, if the decimal point is moved only 1 place to the right, the exponent is 1. However, an exponent of 1 is often not written since any number raised to the first power is equal to itself and $10^1 = 10$. The number 56 expressed in scientific notation is $5.6 * 10^1$, expressed as simply $5.6 * 10$.

Properties of Logarithms

Certain operations with logarithms are of importance. They include the following:

log 10^a	= a log 10
log (a * b)	= log a + log b
log (a ÷ b)	= log a – log b

When the logarithm of a value is sought, the problem is interpreted as finding the exponent of a number when the number is expressed in scientific form. As such, the logarithm of 154.81 is calculated as follows:

$$\log 154.81$$
converting the value to scientific form
$$= \log (1.5481 * 10^2)$$
$$= \log 1.5481 * \log 10^2$$
$$= \log 1.5481 + (2 * \log 10)$$
$$= \log 1.5481 + (2 * 1)$$
$$= \log 1.5481 + 2$$

Since $10^1 = 1$ and $\log 10 = 1$, it stands to reason that the log of any number less than 10 must be a decimal, which is a value that is less 1. Further, any value that can be expressed in standard notation can be expressed as a multiple of that decimal and an exponent applied to 10. As an example, the value .056 is less than 10 and can be expressed in standard notation as $5.6 * 10^2$. The log of .056 is calculated as follows:

$$\log .056$$
$$= \log\ (5.6 * 10^{-2})$$
$$= \log 5.6 * \log 10^{-2}$$
$$= \log 5.6 + (-2 * \log 10)$$
$$= \log 5.6 + (-2 * 1)$$
$$= \log 5.6 - 2$$

Antilogarithms

The mathematics of logarithms provides methods to compute the log of a value and, conversely, methods of determining the value itself. In the statement $\log .056 = 1.251811973$, the value .056 corresponding to the logarithm is known as the antilogarithm of 1.251811973.

Example:

In the equation $(x-a)^n = b$, we want to solve for n using logarithms.

$$\log (x - a)^n = \log b$$
$$n \log (x - a) = \log b$$
$$\log (x-a) = \frac{\log b}{n}$$
$$x - a = \text{antilog} \left(\frac{\log b}{n} \right)$$
$$x = \text{antilog} \left(\frac{\log b}{n} \right) + a$$

Characteristic and Mantissa

It can be seen from the two examples above that a solution of a logarithm may result in two terms: a logarithm and a whole number. The term that is a whole number is called the characteristic. The characteristic is equal to the power of the number when the number is expressed in scientific form. The term that is a logarithm is called the mantissa. The mantissa is equal to the logarithm of the number between 1 and 10. In the value log $(5.6 * 10^{-2})$, the characteristic is -2 and the mantissa is log 5.6. As such:

$$\log .056$$
$$= \log 5.6 - 2,$$
as was calculated in the example above

The purpose in converting the logarithm of a number into an expression that includes a logarithm of a number is that the logarithm in the new expression seeks the logarithm of a number whose value falls between 1 and 10. As such, the value of the logarithm can be found in a table of logarithms. A much easier method of computing logarithms is to use a calculator or other method of digital computing. The process of using a table of logarithms becomes complicated when the characteristic is negative.

In higher levels of mathematics and engineering than are presented here, logarithms and exponents have application in complex computing, particularly when the notation e is used. This book does not extend to that level of sophistication and, as such, will not delve any further into the complexities of how and why logarithms work. The important thing to know about logarithms and exponents is that they are the methods necessary to solve problems involving square and other roots. In the absence of digital computing, even a low cost scientific calculator provides more timely and accurate results than manual computations.

Linear Equations

A single equation with two unknowns is known as a linear equation. The term linear is used since the geometry of lines dictates that any line can be defined by at least two points .The value of one unknown can be stated in terms of the other unknown. As an example, $2x + y = 48$ is a linear equation with unknowns x and y. The value of x may be stated as follows:

$$2x + y = 48$$
$$2x = 48 - y$$
$$x = (48 - y) \div 2$$

Likewise, the value of y may be stated as follows:

$$2x + y = 48$$
$$y = 48 - 2x$$

Thus, for each x, there is a corresponding y to form pairs of solutions.

x =	0	1	-1	2	-2	3	-3	...
y =	48	46	50	44	52	42	54	...

When these pairs of solutions are plotted on a chart, they form a straight line as follows:

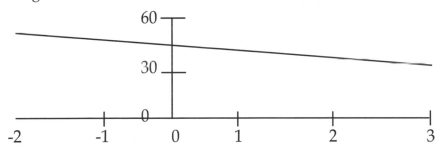

The equation of a line is $y = mx+b$, where x and y are coordinate points, m is the slope of the line, and b is the distance above or below x = 0 where the line crosses the y-axis. The line defined by $y = -2x + 48$ has a slope of -2, and it crosses the y-axis at x = 0 and y = 48.

Simultaneous Linear Equations

When two or more linear equations are satisfied by the same set of values, the equations are called simultaneous linear equations.

Example:

An investor invests $40,000 in three different properties that yield $1,494 in profit in the first year. The distribution of the profits was $3(\frac{1}{2})\%$, $3(\frac{3}{4})\%$, and 4%. One-fourth of the investment amount was invested in the property that yielded the least amount of profit. We want to determine how much was invested in the other two properties.

Let x = the amount invested in property x at $3(\frac{1}{2})\%$
Let y = the amount invested in property y at $3(\frac{3}{4})\%$
Let z = the amount invested in property z at 4%

Since the total investment was distributed among the three properties, the relationship between the individual properties and the investment amount is defined as:

$$x + y + z = \$40,000$$

$\frac{1}{4}$ of the investment amount was invested in property x, so

$$x = \frac{1}{4} * \$40,000$$
$$= \$10,000$$

and the relationship is redefined as:

$$\$10,000 + y + z = \$40,000$$
$$y + z = \$30,000$$

Since the total profit was acquired from all three properties, the relationship between the properties and profit is defined as:

$$3(\tfrac{1}{2})\%x + 3(\tfrac{3}{4})\%y + 4\%z = \$1,494$$

Using the table of equivalents, we know that

$$\frac{1}{2}\% = 50\% \text{ and}$$
$$3(\tfrac{1}{2})\% = 3.5\%$$
also,
$$\frac{3}{4}\% = 75\% \text{ and}$$
$$3(\tfrac{3}{4})\% = 3.75\%$$

The relationship is redefined as:

$$.035x + .0375y + .04z = \$1{,}494$$
$$(.035 * \$10{,}000) + .0375y + .04z = \$1{,}494$$
$$350 + .0375y + .04z = \$1{,}494$$
$$.0375y + .04z = \$1{,}144$$

We now have two simultaneous linear equations with two unknowns:

$$y + z = \$30{,}000$$
$$.0375y + .04z = \$1{,}144$$

To solve such equations, we must eliminate one of the unknowns and find the value of the remaining unknown. Once the value of this unknown is found, it is substituted in either of the original equations to find the value of the other unknown.

If the numerical coefficients of one unknown are the same and have like signs, subtracting one equation from the other eliminates the unknown in those equations. If the numerical coefficients are the same but have different signs, adding the two equations eliminates the unknown. If the numerical coefficients are not the same, decide which unknown is to be eliminated. Multiply the first equation by the coefficient of the unknown to be eliminated in the second equation, and multiply the second equation by the coefficient of the unknown to be eliminated in the first equation.

$$y + z = \$30{,}000$$
$$.0375y + .04z = \$1{,}144$$

The coefficients of the unknowns are not the same. A decision is made to eliminate z using the coefficient 0.4 in the second equation to cancel z in the first equation.

$$0.4 * (y + z = \$30,000)$$
$$0.4y + 0.4z = \$30,000$$

We now have two equations with the same numerical coefficients of the unknown and like signs. The equations are subtracted to eliminate z:

$$0.375y + 0.4z = \$1,144$$
$$- (0.4y + 0.4z = \$30,000)$$
$$\overline{-.0025\ y \qquad\quad = -\$56}$$
$$y = \$22,400$$

So,
$$y = \$22,400$$

Substituting the value of y in the first equation, we solve for z:

$$y + z = \$30,000$$
$$\$22,400 + z = \$30,000$$
$$z = \$30,000 - \$22,400$$
$$z = \$7,600$$

The investor invested $22,400 in property y at 3(3/4)% and $7,600 in property z at 4%.

An alternative method of finding a solution involves solving for one unknown in terms of the other unknown in one of the equations and then substituting the calculated value for the same unknown in the other equation. This creates an equation in one unknown, which can be solved. When one of the equations is solved, the result is substituted in the other equation to solve for the second unknown. Using the previous example:

$$y + z = \$30,000$$
$$.0375y + .04z = \$1,494$$

Solve for y in the first equation:

$$y + z = \$30,000$$
$$y = \$30,000 - z$$

Substitute this value of x in the second equation:

$$.0375y + .04z = \$1,144$$
$$.0375 * (\$30,000 - z) + .04z = \$1,144$$
$$\$1,125 - .0375z + .04z = \$1,144$$
$$\$1,125 - .0025z = \$1,144$$
$$.0025z = \$19$$
$$z = \$7,600$$

Substitute this value in the first equation:

$$y + z = \$30,000$$
$$y + \$7,600 = \$30,000$$
$$y = \$22,400$$

Linear Equations in More Than Two Unknowns

When a system of linear equations involves more than two unknowns, the process of solving for unknowns is the same. Whether there are three equations in three unknowns or four equations in four unknowns, the objective is to eliminate one of the unknowns in favor of the others and to continue this procedure until there are only two equations in two unknowns. The values for the other unknowns are then found by substituting the values in the original equations. Though this is a lengthy process, it is not complex.

Example:

Jack assumes the role of property manager and records show that, over the past three years, purchases of supplies were made from a specific wholesaler. The records show discounts applied to bulk purchases, but it does not show the discount applied to the individual items. Jack needs to itemize the cost of each item to access the discount applied to each item purchased.

Year	Number of Items Purchased			Discount
	Hinges	Keys	Locks	
1	10,000	5,000	2,000	$8,400
2	8,000	6,000	3,000	$7,900
3	9,000	4,000	4,000	$6,500

$$(1)\ 10{,}000x + 5{,}000y + 2{,}000z = \$8{,}400$$
$$(2)\ 8{,}000x + 6{,}000y + 3{,}000z = \$7{,}900$$
$$(3)\ 9{,}000x + 4{,}000y + 4{,}000z = \$6{,}500$$

Each of these equations could be reduced by dividing each term by 100 to eliminate two zeros from each term of each equation.

$$(1)\ 100x + 50y + 20z = \$84$$
$$(2)\ 80x + 60y + 30z = \$79$$
$$(3)\ 90x + 40y + 40z = \$65$$

It is determined that z will be the first term to be eliminated. We did not have to choose z; we could just as well have chosen x or y to be eliminated first. To eliminate z, equation (1) will be multiplied by 2 and subtracted from equation (3). Multiplying equation (1) by 2 ensures that the coefficient of z in equation (1) is the same as the coefficient of z in equation (3). Since the signs of the terms involving z are the same, equation (1) is subtracted from equation (3).

$$(1)\ 200x + 100y + 40z = \$168$$
$$(3)\ 90x + 40y + 40z = \$65$$
$$\overline{\hphantom{(3)}\ (4)\ 110x + 60y \hphantom{+ 40z} = \$103}$$

Now, to eliminate z in equation (2), equation (2) will be multiplied by 4, and equation (3) will be multiplied times 3 and then subtracted from equation (2).

$$(2)\ 320x + 240y + 120z = \$316$$
$$(3)\ 270x + 120y + 120z = \$195$$
$$(5)\ 50x + 120\ y \qquad\quad = \$121$$

We have eliminated the unknown, z, and created two new equations in two unknowns, namely equations (4) and (5). We now need to eliminate one of the other unknowns. Using the equations that were generated in eliminating z, we have two equations in two unknowns, x and y. Once we solve for one of these unknowns, we can apply substitution to find the other unknown. We choose to eliminate the unknown y. Equation (4) will be multiplied by 2 and subtracted from equation (5):

$$(5)\ 50x + 120\ y = \$121$$
$$(4)\ 220x + 120y = \$206$$
$$170x \qquad\quad = \$85$$
$$\text{and } x = \$0.5 = 50 \text{ cents}$$

We have now eliminated the unknown y, and we have a value for the unknown, x = $0.5. Substituting x in equation (4), we obtain the following value for y:

$$110x + 60y = \$103$$
$$110(\$0.5) + 60y = \$103$$
$$60y = \$103 - \$55$$
$$y = \$48 \div 60$$
$$y = \$0.8 = 80 \text{ cents}$$

Substituting x and y in equation (1), we obtain the following value for z:

$$10{,}000x + 5{,}000y + 2{,}000z = \$8{,}400$$
$$10{,}000(\$0.5) + 5{,}000(\$0.8) + 2{,}000z = \$8{,}400$$
$$2{,}000z = \$8{,}400 - \$4{,}000 - \$5{,}000$$
$$2{,}000z = -\$\$600$$
$$z = -\$0.3 = -30 \text{ cents}$$

The discount per item is:

X = 50 cents per hinge
Y = 80 cents per lock
Z = -30 cents per key

The wholesaler does not provide a discount on keys.

Quadratic Equations

A quadratic equation is an equation in which, in its simplest form, the highest power of any unknown term is in the form of a square (as in x^2). Quadratic equations are also called equations of the second degree. The equation $4x^2 + 9 = 3x^2 - 15$ is a quadratic equation, since the highest power of any unknown is a square. Since all unknowns of the equation are square, the equation is considered a pure or incomplete quadratic. The equation, $x^2 + x + 4$ contains both a square and a power of the first degree. This equation is considered a complete quadratic.

An incomplete quadratic equation is solved for the unknown using the following steps:

- Simplify the equation to the form $ax^2 - b = 0$.

- Isolate the unknown term (x^2) to one side of the equation.

- Extract the square root of both sides of the equation.

The square root calculation results in roots as solutions that may be either positive or negative since the square root of $x^2 = \pm x$. Each of these roots must be substituted in the equation to determine which root actually satisfies the equation. As an example, the solution to $4x^2 + 9 = 3x^2 - 15$ is calculated as follows:

$$4x^2 + 9 = 3x^2 - 15$$
$$4x^2 - 3x^2 = -15 - 9$$

$$x^2 = -24$$
$$x = \pm \sqrt{-24}$$
$$x = \pm \sqrt{(4 * 6)}$$
$$x = \pm 2 \sqrt{6}$$

If $x = 2 \sqrt{6}$
$$4x^2 + 9 = 3x^2 - 15$$
$$(4 * 4 * 6) + 9 = (3 * 4 * 6) - 15$$
$$96 + 9 = 72 - 15$$
$$105 \neq 57$$

If $x = -2 \sqrt{6}$
$$4x^2 + 9 = 3x^2 - 15 =$$
$$(4 * -4 * 6) + 9 = (3 * -4 * 6) - 15$$
$$-96 + 9 = -72 - 15$$
$$-87 = -87$$

So, $x = -2 \sqrt{6}$

Complete quadratic equations may be solved by factoring. The process is as follows:

- Move all terms of the equation to the left hand side of the equation and set the equation equal to zero.

- Factor the left hand side of the equation.

- Let each term containing an unknown be set equal to zero.

- Solve each of the resulting equations.

As an example, the solution for the complete quadratic equation $4x^2 - 2x = 3x^2 + 8$ is as follows:

$$4x^2 - 2x = 3x^2 + 8$$
$$4x^2 - 2x - 3x^2 - 8 = 0$$
$$x^2 - 2x - 8 = 0$$
$$(x + 2)(x - 4) = 0$$

Let $x + 2 = 0$, then
$$x = -2$$
and substituting $x = -2$ in the original equation yields:
$$4(4) + 4 = 3(4) + 8$$
$$16 + 4 = 12 + 8$$
$$20 = 20$$

Let $x - 4 = 0$, then
$$x = 4$$
and substituting $x = -4$ in the original equation yields:
$$4(16) + 8 = 3(16) + 8$$
$$64 + 8 = 48 + 8$$
$$72 \neq 56$$

So, $x = -2$ and $x \neq 4$.

The Quadratic Formula

Any quadratic equation may be expressed by the quadratic formula $ax^2 + bx + c = 0$, where a is the coefficient of the quadratic term, b is the coefficient of the linear term, and c is not unknown.

The solution to any quadratic equation is solved using the following quadratic formula:

$$x = \frac{-b \pm \sqrt{b^2 - 4ac}}{2a}$$

The equation $x + 3 = 72 \div (x - 3)$ can be expressed as a quadratic equation as follows:

$$x + 3 = \frac{72}{x - 3}$$
$$(x + 3)(x - 3) = 72$$
$$x^2 - 3x + 3x - 9 = 72$$
$$x^2 - 81 = 0$$

The term involving x is equal to 0, such that $b = 0$.

The equation is solved as follows:

$$x = \frac{-b \pm \sqrt{b^2 - 4ac}}{2a}$$

$$x = \frac{-0 \pm \sqrt{0 - (4*1*81)}}{2*1}$$

$$= \frac{\pm \sqrt{-324}}{2}$$

$$= \frac{\pm 18}{2}$$

$$= \pm 9$$

Measurements

Physical measurements have many applications in real estate and are essential in identifying properties and assessing the property value.

Measuring Surface and Space

Problems involving measurements are an integral part of real estate. Computations of acreage, footage, and other such measurements are necessary. Some of the most commonly used units of measure include inches, feet, and yards. Some of the less familiar units of measure may include chain, rod, and mile. Units used in measuring surfaces and space and their equivalents are as follows:

1 foot	= 12 inches
1 yard	= 3 feet
1 chain	= 66 feet
1 rod	= 16(1/2) feet
1 mile	= 5,280 feet

Linear Measures

The measurement of space may include linear measurements, area measurements, or volume measurements. Linear measurements measure the distance from one point to another. Linear measurements may be expressed using any of the units of measure indicated above.

3-D Linear Measures

An investment may involve property or some other commodity that occupies surface and space. The amount of surface or space that is occupied is usually identified by coordinates or by volume. Coordinates of a coordinate system are used to measure the length, width, and height of an object. Length is often assigned the value of x, width is often assigned the value of y, and height is often assigned the value of z. However, this assignment of coordinates is not absolute. Different individuals may define coordinates differently. The point is that an object must have at least two coordinate points to able to be defined on a surface and at least three coordinate points to be defined in space. Land is often measured by its width and length since its height is often defined as all space above and below the area defined by measured coordinates. In most land measurements, the z coordinate is equal to infinity. However, any structure placed on a parcel of land is likely to have some defined vertical measurement (or z coordinate).

Area Measures

Area measurement involves the measurement of surfaces. Some of the most commonly used units of area measurement and their equivalents include the following:

1 square foot	= 1 foot * 1 foot = 144 square inches
1 square yard	= 9 square feet = 3 feet * 3 feet
1 square mile	= 1 mile * 1 mile

1 acre	= 160 *sq* yards
	= 43,560 square feet
1 square mile	= 640 acres
	= 1 section
1 section	= 640 acres
1 township	= 36 sections

Areas are expressed in square feet. The formulae for determining area are as follows:

The area of any square or rectangle	$= L * W$	L = Length W = Width
The area of any triangle	$= \frac{1}{2} * B * Alt$	B = Base Alt = Altitude
The area of any circle	$= \pi * R^2$	π = pi R^2 = radius squared
The area of any trapezoid	$= \frac{a + b}{2} * h$	a = length of one side b = length of other side h = height

Volume Measures

Volume measures are an extension of area measures. Volume measures add dimension and height (or depth) to area measurements. Some common units of volume measures and their equivalents are as follows:

1 cubic foot	= 1 foot * 1 foot ˣ 1 foot
	= 1,728 cubic inches
1 cubic yard	= 27 cubic feet
	= 3 feet * 3 feet * 3 feet

The formulae for determining volume are as follows:

| The area of any rectangle or cube | = Length * Width * Height | $= L * W * H$ |

The area of any triangular or cylindrical object	= Area * Height	= A * H
The area of any prism	= 1/2 (Base * Height * Width)	= 1/2 (B * H * W)

Directional Measures

Circles are the basis for directional measurements.

Circle	= 360 degrees
1 degree	= 60 minutes
1 minute	= 60 seconds
1 quadrant	= 90 degrees

Measuring Time

There are instances when periods of time will need to be measured. By expressing the beginning date and ending date of a time period in terms of year, month, and day, the elapsed period of time may be calculated. For example, the date of June 16, 1982 is expressed as 82-6-16. The date of March 25, 2006 is expressed as 06-3-25. The two dates should then be written with the earlier date placed beneath the later date as follows:

$$
\begin{array}{ccc}
2006 & 3 & 25 \\
1982 & 6 & 16
\end{array}
$$

The earlier date is then subtracted from the later date. However, in our example, 6 months cannot be subtracted from 3 months. So, we take one from the year 2006 and add it to the months, such that the number of months is changed from 3 to 3 + 12 = 15, and the year changes from 2006 to 2005. The subtraction proceeds as follows:

$$
\begin{array}{ccc}
2005 & 15 & 25 \\
- \ 1982 & 6 & 16 \\
\hline
23 & 9 & 9
\end{array}
$$

The calculated time period is 23 years, 9 months, and 9 days.

Solving Problems

Problems in business and finance are not necessarily algebraic equations, but certain relationships are established from known facts. These relationships can then be stated as algebraic equations with the use of symbols, such as "x" or "a" to represent an unknown quantity. After a problem has been defined by equations, it is possible to readily solve the problem.

The ability to express algebraic relationships assists in developing an individual's capacity for business reasoning and the understanding of business processes. While an individual that is not able to develop algebraic relationships may be quite capable of applying a specific formula, the individual that understands the wider implications of the procedures involved in the formula may be better capable to find a quicker solution or find a solution when the problem differs, however slight, from the problem for which a formula was designed to address.

Percentage Problems

The three basic arithmetic percentage problems discussed under "Arithmetic" may be easily expressed as equations when presented in certain form. Recall that the three basic percentage problems include finding the rate, percent of a number, and base. Using a substitution of mathematical terms for English terms, such problems may be expressed as algebraic equations. The substitutions are as follows:

- Convert the term "**is**" to the mathematical symbol "="
- Convert the term "**what**" to the unknown variable "**x**"
- Convert the term "**of**" to the mathematical symbol "*"
- Convert the term "**percent**" to the mathematical symbol "%"

These substitutions are applied to problem statements to form mathematical equations as shown in Table 2.

TABLE 2: CONVERTING PERCENTAGE PROBLEMS INTO MATHEMATICAL EQUATIONS		
Basic Percentage Problems	English Problem Statement	Mathematical Equation
Finding the Rate	20 is what percent of 60?	$20 = x\% * 60$
Finding the Percent of a Number	What is 20% of 60?	$x = 20\% * 60$
Finding the Base	20 is 60% of what?	$20 = 60\% * x$

Not all conversions from word problems to equations are so simple. Most conversions will require more thought. A clear understanding of the problem and the possible mathematical interpretations of the problem are necessary.

Percentage problems are of importance since the real world problems for which they are used are often confusing. The problem stems from determining the proper relationships between the base, rate, and the number under consideration. If any two of these values are known, the other value may be found once an appropriate problem statement is formed and substitutions are made.

Example 1:

We seek to find the percent of profit for an item that cost $100 and is then sold for $110. Some people are likely to indicate 10% since there is a profit of $10. However, profit and the percent of profit are two differing mathematical concepts. Profit is the amount made over and above the cost. Profit is expressed as a dollar amount. However, the percent of profit is that part of the cost that is profit. Percent of profit is expressed as a percentage. Recall that :

Is	implies	=
What	implies	x
Of	implies	*
Percent	implies	%

The problem statement is:

What percentage of the cost is the profit?

Substituting mathematical terms for English terms, the problem becomes:

$$x\% * \text{the cost} = \text{the profit}$$
$$x\% = \text{the profit} \div \text{the cost}$$
$$= \$10 \div \$100$$
$$= 0.1$$
$$= 10\%$$

The profit is 10% of the cost.

Example 2:

If instead the problem involved determining what part of the selling price was the cost, the problem statement would be:

What percent of the selling price is the cost?

$$x\% * \text{the selling price} = \text{the cost}$$
$$x\% = \text{the cost} \div \text{the selling price}$$
$$= \$100 \div \$110$$
$$= 0.909$$
$$= 90.9\%$$

The cost is 90.9% of the selling price.

Example 3:

If the problem involved determining what part the selling price was of the cost, the problem statement would be:

What percent of the cost is the selling price?

$$x\% * \text{the cost} = \text{the selling price}$$
$$x\% = \text{the selling price} \div \text{the cost}$$

$$= \$110 \div \$100$$
$$= 1.1$$
$$x = 110\%$$

The selling price is 110% of the cost.

Clearly, one must first be able to properly define the relationship of the variables to develop a problem statement and then solve the mathematical statement. Making the same type of substitutions of English terms for mathematical terms the solutions to the previous three examples may be easily checked as follows:

The profit is 10% of the cost.

$$\$10 = 10\% * \$100$$
$$\$10 = .10 * \$100$$
$$\$10 = \$10$$

The cost is 90.9% of the selling price.

$$\$100 = 90.9\% * \$110$$
$$\$100 = .909 * 110$$
$$\$100 = \$100$$

The selling price is 110% of the cost.

$$\$110 = 110\% * \$100$$
$$\$110 = 1.1 * 100$$
$$\$110 = \$110$$

The substitutions are applicable to any problem involving percentages. Other examples are as follows:

Example 4:

A home was listed for $175,000 and sold for 90% of the list price. We want to determine the sale price of the home.

The problem statement is:

90% of $175,000 is what?

$$.90 * 175{,}000 = x$$
$$x = \$157{,}500$$

The sale price of the home is $157,500.

Example 5:

A firm's top selling salesperson sold 132 of the 486 homes sold last year. We want to determine the percent of sales by the top selling salesperson. The problem statement is:

132 is what percent of 486?

$$132 = x\% * 486$$
$$x\% = 132 \div 486$$
$$x\% = 0.271$$
$$x = 27.1\%$$

Proportion Problems

Proportion is a measure of the equality of two ratios. A ratio is simply a fraction. A commonly used proportion is the reduction of a fraction to its lowest terms. As an example, the ratio, $25 \div 15 = 5 \div 3$, is a proportion involving four terms: 25, 15, 5, and 3. A proportion always involves four terms. Using a substitution of mathematical terms for English terms, proportion problems may be expressed as algebraic equations. The substitutions are as follows:

- Convert the phrase "**is to**" to the mathematical symbol "÷"

- Convert the phrase "**as**" to the unknown variable "="

These substitutions are applied to the problem statement to form mathematical equations as shown in Table 3.

TABLE 3: CONVERTING PROPORTION PROBLEMS INTO MATHEMATICAL EQUATIONS		
Basic Proportion Problem	English Problem Statement	Mathematical Equation
Find the proportion	a is to b as c is to d	$a \div b = c \div d$

The relationship among proportions provides for any one of the four terms to be determined if any three of the four terms is known. If it is known that the value 4 is to the value 13 as the value 200 is to some unknown value, then let the unknown term be assigned the value x. The value of x may be calculated as follows:

$$\frac{4}{13} = \frac{200}{x}$$

$$x * \frac{4}{13} = 200$$

$$x = 200 * \frac{13}{4}$$

$$x = 650$$

Example 1:

It took 9 men one day to dig 24 cubic yards of dirt to create the foundation for the basement of a house. A new house is being built that requires 80 cubic yards to be dug in two days. We need to determine how many men are necessary.

9 men are to 24 cubic yards as x men are to 80 cubic yards.

The proportion is solved as follows:

$$\frac{9}{24} = \frac{x}{80}$$

$$x = \frac{9}{24} (80)$$

$$x = 30 \text{ men}$$

This proportion is based on only one day. The dirt for the new house is to be dug in two days. As such, we assign the value x_1 to the number of men required for 1 day and x_2 be the number of men required for two days. We then divide x_1 by 2.

$$x_2 = x_1 \div 2$$
$$x_2 = 30 \div 2$$
$$x_2 = 15 \text{ men}$$

Example 2:

A lot is divided into three parts. $1/_3$ of the lot is used for building development, $1/_8$ of the lot is cultivated, and the remaining 125 acres is unused. We want to determine the total acreage of the lot.

The total acreage of the lot is 100% of the lot. Using the equivalences at Table 1, we determine that $1/_3$ of the lot is $33(1/_3)\%$ and $1/_8$ is $12(½)\%$ of the lot. The remaining percentage is:

$$100\% - 33(1/_3)\% - 12(1/_2)\%$$
$$100\% - 33.3\% - 12.5\%$$
$$= 54.2\%$$

Since 125 acres is 54.2% of the lot, we need to determine the acreage of the remaining 45.8% of the lot.

The proportion is:

125 acres is to 54.2% as x acres is to 45.8%

$$\frac{125}{54.2\%} = \frac{x}{45.8\%}$$

$$x = \frac{125}{.542}(.458)$$

$$x = 105.6 \text{ acres}$$

The total acreage of the lot is:

$$105.6 \text{ acres} + 125 \text{ acres}$$
$$= 230.6 \text{ acres}$$

Continued Proportion

Proportions are not always expressed as a ratio. If a proportional relationship involves more than two numbers, the method of distribution must be stated in the form of a continued proportion, such as 2:4:8. A continued proportion allows an amount to be distributed in a series of proportions. The 2:4:8 notation indicates that 2 parts are to be distributed to one member, 4 parts are to be distributed to another member, and 8 parts are to be distributed to a final member. The method for distributing an amount in proportion to a given series of numbers is as follows:

- Find the sum of the numbers in the series.

- Divide the amount by this sum.

- Multiply each number in the series by the resulting quotient.

Example 1:

Three partners decide to distribute profits according to the proportion 5:3:4. The profit of $14,400 is to be distributed to partner X in 5 parts, to partner Y in 3 parts, and to partner Z in 4 parts. The profit must be divided into 12 parts since 5 + 3 + 4 = 12.

$$\$14,400 \div 12 = \$1,200$$
$$\text{Partner X's share} = 5 * \$1,200 = \$6,000$$
$$\text{Partner Y's share} = 3 * \$1,200 = \$3,600$$
$$\text{Partner Z's share} = 4 * \$1,200 = \$4,800$$

ELEMENTARY STATISTICS

Statistics provide a method of describing findings, making estimations, and making decisions. Statistics is the collection, classification, presentation, and interpretation of numerical data. All statistics are based on a population, which is a collection or set of individuals, objects, or measurements. Any subset of the population is known as a sample. Characteristics of a population are known as parameters and numerical characteristics of a sample are called statistics.

Average

There are many situations where the average (or mean) of some quantity will be sought. The arithmetic average of a series of values is calculated by adding all the values together and then dividing the sum by the total number of values. If the number of values in the series is represented as n and x_1 represents the first value in the series, x_2 represents the second value in the series,... and x_n represents the last value of the series, then the average is calculated as:

$$avg = (x_1 + x_2 + x_3 \ldots + x_3) \div n$$

The sum of all the data points is denoted as $\sum x$. The average is denoted as follows:

$$avg = \sum x \div n$$

Example:

The average of the five values 98, 76, 45, 78, and 48 is calculated as follows:

$$98 + 76 + 45 + 78 + 48 = 345$$
$$345 \div 5$$
$$= 69$$

Measures of Dispersion

In statistics, several different measures are used to specify the spread or dispersion of data. The range, average deviation, variance, and standard deviation provide differing measures of dispersion that assist in describing a population of data.

Range

The range of data is a measure of the dispersion that measures the difference between the largest value and the smallest value in a set of data. These large and small values are also called the high and low values. Using the preceding example, the range is calculated as follows:

$$\text{Range} = H - L$$
$$= 98 - 45$$
$$= 53$$

The range indicates that the five values fall with 53 units, if measured on a number line.

Average Deviation

The average deviation is a measure of the dispersion of data about the average value. The dispersion of data about the average value is simply a measure of how far data points are from the average value, as measured on a number line. An individual data point is assigned the value x. The value of x deviates from the average value by an amount equal to $x_D = x - avg$. The deviation is 0 if the data point happens to be equal to the average value. The data point is positive if it is greater than the average value and negative if it is less than the average value. Using the same data sample, the deviation (x_D) of each individual data point is calculated by subtracting the average value from the value of the data point.

$$x_D = x - avg, \text{ for all } x$$

x	avg	x_D
98	- 69 =	29
76	- 69 =	7
45	- 69 =	-24
78	- 69 =	9
48	- 69 =	-21
$\sum (x - avg) =$		0

The sum of all deviations should equal zero. However, the sum of the absolute values of all the individual deviations provides an average deviation from the average value as follows:

$$| x - avg |, \text{ for all } x$$

$$|29| = 29$$
$$|7| = 7$$
$$|-24| = 24$$
$$|9| = 9$$
$$|-21| = 21$$
$$\sum |x-avg| = 90$$

The average deviation from the average value is:

$$(\sum | x - avg |) \div n$$
$$= 90 \div 5$$
$$= 18$$

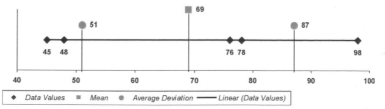

Population, Mean and Average Deviation

Variance

The average deviation is rarely used, but it indicates the average distance that each data point is located from the average value. The more widely used measure of dispersion is variance. The variance provides a measure of the spread of all the data about the average value. The variance (s^2) is calculated as:

$$s^2 = \frac{\sum (x - avg)^2}{n - 1}$$

x - avg	$(x - avg)^2$
29	841
7	49
-24	576
9	81
-21	441
$\sum (x - avg)^2 =$	1988

$$s^2 = \sum (x - avg)^2 \div (n - 1)$$
$$= 1{,}988 \div 4$$
$$= 497$$

The variance may also be expressed as follows:

$$s^2 = \frac{n\sum x^2 - (\sum x)^2}{n(n-1)}$$

x	x^2
98	9604
76	5776
45	2025
78	6084
48	2304
$\sum x = 345$	$\sum x^2 = 25793$

$$= \frac{5(25793) \quad - \quad (345)^2}{5(5 - 1)}$$

$$= \frac{128965 \quad - \quad 119025}{20}$$

$$= \frac{9940}{20}$$

$$= \quad 497$$

The variance is a statistic that is used to compare one set of data with another. The larger the variance, the more dispersed the data.

Standard Deviation

Another widely used measure of dispersion is the standard deviation. The standard deviation is the positive square root of the variance, calculated as follows:

$$s = \sqrt{(s^2)}$$
$$= \sqrt{497}$$
$$= 22.29$$

The standard deviation is also used to compare sets of data with one another. It also forms the basis for two important statistical principles: Chebyshev's theorem and the empirical rule. Chebyshev's theorem dictates that the proportion of any distribution of data, which lies within k standard deviations of the mean, is at least $1 - (1 \div k^2)$, where k is any positive number greater than 1. From our example with k = 22.29, this theorem provides that:

$$1 - (1 \div k^2)$$
$$= 1 - [1 \div (22.29)^2]$$
$$= 1 - (1 \div 497)$$
$$= 1 - .002012$$
$$= 0.997988$$

At least 99.8% of the data falls within 22.29 standard deviations of the mean.

When data from a population is plotted on a histogram bar chart and the data is bunched around the mean and dispersed in both directions, the data is said to have an approximately normal distribution. The data points become more dispersed the further they are away from the mean. The empirical rule dictates that, if a variable is normally distributed, approximately 68% of the data will fall within one standard deviation of the mean; approximately 95% of the data will fall within two standard deviations of the mean, and about 99.7% of the data will fall within three standard deviations of the mean.

Probability

Probability is the relative frequency with which an event can be expected to occur. The probability that an event will occur may be measured empirically, theoretically, or subjectively. The empirical measure is based on experimentation or an observed relative frequency. Theoretical measures are based on the likelihood that one event is just as likely to occur as another. Subjective measures are based on intelligence and prior knowledge.

Empirical Measures

The probability P(A) of an event A occurring in n trials is determined using the formula:

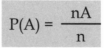

$$P(A) = \frac{nA}{n}$$

where nA is the number of times that event A actually occurred.

Example 1:

In tossing a coin, the number of times for which heads will turn up and the number of times for which tails will turn up may be observed. In an experiment, a single coin is tossed and heads turned up in 104 out of 200 tosses. The observed empirical probability for the occurrence of heads is:

$$P(\text{heads}) = \text{number of heads} \div \text{number of trials}$$
$$= 104 \div 200$$
$$= 0.52$$
$$= 52\%$$

Example 2:

A jar contains a red (R), yellow (Y), and green (G) marble. Two marbles are drawn from the jar and the probability of drawing a red marble is defined as P(R). The possible outcomes are called a sample space. The sample space includes six possibilities as follows:

RY	RG
YR	YG
GR	GY

$$P(R) = \text{number of times that R was drawn} \div \text{sample size}$$
$$= 4 \div 6$$
$$= {}^2/_3$$

If the jar contains a mixture of red (R), yellow (Y), and green (G) marbles and two marbles are drawn from the jar, the probability of drawing a red marble is based on nine possible outcomes as follows:

RR	RY	RG
YY	YR	YG
GG	GR	GY

$$P(R)$$
$$= {}^5/_9$$

In the preceding example, it is assumed that the jar had more than three marbles to choose from and that one colored marble was just as likely to be selected as the other.

Theoretical Measures

If the jar in the preceding example contained exactly 20 red marbles, 10 yellow marbles, and 15 green marbles, one particular colored marble is not as likely to be drawn from the jar as another. Since there are more red marbles than yellow or green, a red marble is more likely to be drawn. Likewise, since there are less yellow marbles than red or green, a yellow marble is less likely to be drawn. The theoretical probability of drawing the different colored marbles is calculated as:

P(any one color) = number of marbles of a particular color ÷ total number of marbles

$$P(R) = 20/45$$
$$P(Y) = 10/45$$
$$P(G) = 15/45$$

Subjective Measures

Subjective measures are used to measure probability when equally likely events do not occur and no experiment has been or can be performed. The precipitation given in a weather forecast, for example, is a subjective probability where events are not equally likely to occur and no experiment can be performed to assign probability. Subjective probability is assigned based on personal judgment. The accuracy of such subjective probability is dependent upon one's ability to correctly evaluate a situation.

In subjective probability, such personal judgment is expressed as a likelihood where the probability is assigned a numerical value between zero and one, with zero indicating that an event cannot or will not occur and one indicating that the event occurs every time.

Further, the probability of all possible outcomes is equal to one.

$$0 \le P(A) \le 1$$
$$\sum P(A) = 1 \text{ for all outcomes}$$

Example:

A weather forecaster indicates from personal judgment that it is eight times more likely to snow as to not snow. The sample space includes the probability of events: snow P(s) and no snow P(ns). The probability of all likely outcomes must be equal to one. So,

$$P(s) + P(ns) = 1$$

The subjective probability as defined by the forecaster is:

$$P(s) = 8 * P (ns)$$
Since P(s) + P(ns) = 1, we substitute for P(s), such that:
$$P(s) + P(ns) = 1$$
$$8 * P(ns) + P(ns) = 1$$
$$9\, P(ns) = 1$$
$$P(ns) = {}^1/_9$$

Substituting the value of P (ns) in the original equation, we find the P(s):

$$P(s) = 8 * P(ns)$$
$$= 8 * {}^1/_9$$
$$= {}^8/_9$$

The total sample space P(s) + P(ns) = 1 and $({}^1/_9) + ({}^8/_9) = {}^9/_9 = 1$.

Compound Probabilities

Compound probability combines several events. They include complementary events, mutually exclusive events, independent events, and dependent events.

Complementary Events

The complement of the event A is the set of samples in a sample space that do not belong to event A. The complement of event A is denoted as A' and the probability of event A' is denoted as P(A)'. For any given event, the following holds true:

$$P(A)' + P(A) = 1$$
$$\text{and}$$
$$P(A)' = 1 - P(A)$$

Example:

The probability of a selling a home in a newly established development within the next month is determined to be 76%. The probability of a sale is represented as P(A) = 0.76. As such, the probability of not selling is represented as P(A)' and is calculated as follows:

$$P(A)' = 1 - P(A)$$
$$= 1 - 0.76$$
$$= 0.24$$

Mutually Exclusive Events

Mutually exclusive events are events where one event precludes the occurrence of other events. In short, if one event occurs, others cannot occur. For example, if the event is the pulling of a ball from a hat, only one ball is selected. It cannot be both red and some other color at the same time. The probability of selecting a red ball and the probability of selecting a green ball are mutually exclusive events.

The compound probability of event A or event B occurring is represented as P(A or B), where A and B are mutually exclusive events. The probability is determined as:

$$P(A \text{ or } B) = P(A) + P(B)$$
and
$$P(A \text{ or } B \text{ or } \ldots \text{or } G) = P(A) + P(B) + \ldots + P(G)$$

Independent and Dependent Events

Independent events are events where the occurrence, or non-occurrence, of one event does not affect the probability of the other. The compound probability that events A and B will occur is represented as $P(A + B)$, where A and B are independent events.

$$P(A \text{ and } B) = P(A) * P(B)$$
and
$$P(A \text{ and } B \text{ and } \ldots \text{and } G) = P(A) * P(B) * \ldots * P(G)$$

The lack of independence is dependence. The relationship between mutually exclusive, independent, and independent events is summarized as follows:

- If two events are mutually exclusive, they are also dependent events.

- If two events are independent, they are not mutually exclusive.

- If two events are not mutually exclusive, they may be either dependent or independent.

- If two events are dependent, they may be either mutually exclusive or not mutually exclusive.

Conditional Probability

The compound probability that A will occur given that event B has occurred is represented as $P(A \mid B)$ if A and B are independent events.

$$P(A \mid B) = P(A)$$
and
$$P(A \mid B) = P(A \text{ and } B) \div P(B)$$

If A and B are dependent events, then

$$P(A \text{ and } B) = P(A) * P(B \mid A)$$
or
$$P(A \text{ and } B) = P(B) * P(A \mid B)$$

If A and B are not mutually exclusive, then

$$P(A \text{ or } B) = P(A) + P(B) - P(A \text{ and } B)$$

Example:

An investor wants to purchase hazard insurance for his personal residence and his rental property. Historical data suggests that the probability of filing a claim is 4/10 for the rental property and 5/100 for his personal residence. The probability of claims, given that these are independent events, is as follows:

The probability of a claim at both properties is:

$$= P(A \text{ and } B)$$
$$= P(A) * P(B)$$
$$= 0.4 * 0.05$$
$$= 0.02$$

The probability of a claim at neither property is:

$$= P(A \text{ and } B)'$$
$$= P(A)' \text{ and } P(B)'$$
$$= 0.6 * 0.95$$
$$= 0.57$$

The probability of a claim at one of the properties:

$$P(A \text{ or } B)$$

$$= P(A) + P(B)$$
$$= 0.4 + 0.05$$
$$= 0.405$$

Symbolic Logic

Logic is a branch of mathematics that is often overlooked. Logic is concerned with developing one's ability to reason, and reasoning is fundamental to problem solving. Logic is concerned with arguments, which result from inference. Arguments of logic are not to be confused with fighting arguments. An argument in logic is any group of propositions, one of which is claimed to follow from the others, and the others are regarded as providing support or grounds for the truth of the other. Arguments are expressed as statements, and logic presumes that every statement is either true or false. As such, every statement has a truth-value that is either true or false. Further, there are two types of statements: simple and compound. A simple statement is a statement that does not include any other statement. A compound statement is a statement that contains other statements. "The wagon is red," is a simple statement. "The wagon is red and the wagon rolls," is a compound statement.

Symbolic logic provides methods of representing statements of argument with symbols and then determining the truth-value of such statements. Simple statements are either true or false, based on one's perception or interpretation. As such, "The wagon is red" is true if the color of the wagon is red. However, the statement is false if the color of the wagon is blue.

Compound statements can be more complex and require the techniques of symbolic logic to symbolize statements. There are four primary types of compound statements. They include conjunctions, negations, disjunctions, and conditional statements. In symbolizing statements, one cannot merely rely on the placement of words in a statement. One must be capable of interpreting what the statement means and then restate that meaning in symbolic terms.

Arguments

"While poverty exists, the world is not perfect" is a compound statement that may be interpreted to mean, "If the world were perfect, there would be no poverty." Assuming the original statement is true, the following statements are also true:

> Either the world is perfect or poverty exists.

> Unless poverty does not exit, the world cannot be perfect.

Several statements may be combined to form a valid argument, or a valid conclusion may be drawn from several given statements. The statements are called premises (or hypotheses) and a statement of result is called the conclusion. The process of going from premise to conclusion is called deduction. Sometimes the deduction of an argument is simple and other times it is not. A direct argument makes for the simplest type of deduction.

Example:

> Hypothesis: All single-family homes are real property.

> Hypothesis: All real property is real estate.

> Conclusion: Then all single-family homes are real estate.

> This may be easily demonstrated in a diagram.

Deduction is proof, but sometimes such proof is not available and indirect proof must be sought. Using indirect proof of a statement insists that all except a particular one must be false.

Conjunction

A conjunction is a compound statement that contains at least two statements, called conjuncts, and the word, "and." A conjunction with statements, p and q, joined by the word "and" is true if and only if both of its conjuncts are true.

If p is true and q is true	then p and q are true
If p is true and q is false	then p and q are false
If p is false and q is true	then p and q are false
If p is false and q is false	then p and q are false

These statements form the basis for what is called a truth table. A truth table provides a method of representing the truth-values: true and false. The symbol used to represent the term "and" is *. The truth table for a conjunction is as follows:

p	q	p * q
T	T	T
T	F	F
F	T	F
F	F	F

Example:

We are given the statements:

The investor has an income property.

The investor has two properties.

We want to symbolize the argument, "The investor has two income producing properties."

The argument must first be restated to form a compound statement. We only know that one property is income producing. We know nothing about the other property except that it exists. We restate and symbolize the argument as follows:

Let p = the investor has two properties = T

Let q = both properties are income producing = F

Therefore, the investor has two properties and both properties are income producing.

From the truth table, we see that:

$$p * q$$
$$= T * F$$
$$= F$$

Negation

A negation is a statement with the word "not" in it. The negation of a statement may be expressed by prefixing the statement with the phrases, "It is not" or "It is not the case that." The negation of statement p is represented as ~p. The truth table for negation is as follows:

P	~p
T	F
F	T

Example:

Given the statement p = The investor has an income producing property.

We symbolize the statement: The investor does not have an income producing property, as:

~p

Disjunction

A disjunction, also called an alternation, is a compound statement with statements joined by the term the "or." A disjunction is true if at least one conjunct is true. The symbol used to represent the term "or" is v. The truth table for disjunction is as follows:

p	q	p v q
T	T	T
T	F	T
F	T	T
F	F	F

Example:

We are given the statements:

The investor owns an apartment building.

The investor owns a single-family home.

We symbolize the argument: The investor owns neither an apartment building nor a single-family home.

Let p = the investor owns an apartment building = T

Let q = the investor owns a single-family home = T

Therefore, the investor does not own an apartment building nor a single-family home. From the truth table, we see that:

$$= \sim(T \text{ v } T)$$
$$= \sim T$$
$$= F$$

Deductive Reasoning

If A and B represent statements that are true and X and Y represent statements that are false, symbolic logic is used to deduce whether the relationships between the statements are true or false. The following examples make use of truth tables to determine whether the relationship between A, B, and C or A, B, X, and Y are true.

Example:

$$[A \vee (B \vee C)] * [(A \vee B) \vee C]$$
$$= [T \text{ or } (T \text{ or } T)] \text{ and } [(T \text{ or } T) \text{ or } T]$$
$$= (T \text{ or } T) \text{ and } (T \text{ or } T)$$
$$= T \text{ and } T$$
$$= T$$

$$\sim (A \vee Y) * (B \vee X)$$
$$= \text{not } (A \text{ or } Y) \text{ and } (B \text{ or } X)$$
$$= \text{not } (T \text{ or } F) \text{ and } (T \text{ or } F)$$
$$= \text{not } (T \text{ and } T)$$
$$= \text{not } T$$
$$= F$$

Conditional Statements

Conditional statements are compound statements of the form:

If antecedent *then* consequent

In a conditional statement, an antecedent (or implican) is expressed between the terms "if" and "then" and the consequent (or implicate) follows the term "then." A conditional statement asserts that the antecedent implies the consequent. It does not assert that the antecedent is true. However, if the antecedent is true, it follows that the consequent is also true. Likewise, a conditional statement does not assert that the consequent is true. However, the consequent is true if the antecedent is true.

The symbolism used for conditional statements is ⊃, the horseshoe. The conditional statement "if p then q" is represented as p ⊃ q. The truth table for conditional statements is as follows:

p	q	p ⊃ q
T	T	T
T	F	F
F	T	T
F	F	T

Example:

Argument: If the number 2 is less than the number 6, then any number less than 2 is less than 6.

Argument restated: If any number is less than 2, then that number is also less than 6.

Symbolism: If $(x < 2)$ then $(x < 6)$

This equation is true for any value of x as follows:

	Statement	Truth Value
x = 1	If (1 < 2) then (1 < 6)	T ⊃ T = T
x = 2	If (2 < 2) then (2 < 6)	F ⊃ T = T
x = 3	If (3 < 2) then (3 < 6)	F ⊃ T - T
x = -1	If (-1 < 2) then (-1 < 6)	T ⊃ T = T

Inference

Inference involves testing an argument of form for proof of validity or invalidity. The statement p * g is a statement of form because, when statements are substituted for the variables p and q, a statement is formed. This discussion assumes that simple statements are neither logically false nor logically true. When one agrees with the premise of an argument and disagrees with the conclusion, for example, the argument is judged as invalid. Invalidity is proved by the method of logical analogy. If an argument is judged to be invalid, it does not mean there is no formal proof of validity, but a failure to discover formal proof of validity.

This book will not delve into further detail regarding the mathematics of logic, reasoning, and inference. We emphasize, however, that individuals involved in real estate need to have a certain level of reading comprehension to be able to interpret real estate contracts and property listings in order to formulate relevant problem statements and then find solutions to them. Some problems will require numeric computations to find solutions; other problems will require logic and reasoning, while others will involve both disciplines.

Example:

A partial property listing reads as follows:

The house is two-story, of brick construction, located in a residential subdivision of similar homes, built by the same builder at about the same time. There are four large bedrooms on the second floor, plus two bathrooms. There are hardwood floors throughout the first floor except the kitchen, which has a vinyl covering. The entire second floor, including stairs and baths, is carpeted. Owners have added a large below ground swimming pool, plus a bath house containing a sauna, and have had the grounds professionally landscaped at a cost of several thousand dollars. There is an automatic washer and electric dryer in the utility area.

Example 1:

We want to determine if all the bedrooms contain more than 90 square feet.

Let:

p = All rooms of the property are more than 90 square feet.

q = There are 4 large bedrooms.

Therefore, there are 4 large bedrooms, and the rooms are more than 90 feet.

The first premise is true because it may be concluded that 90 square feet represents a small room since 90 ft² represents a room that is about 9 x 10 ft in size, which is a small room by any standard. The second premise is true since it is taken directly from the listing.

So, p = T, q = T and we determine p*q from the truth tables:

$$p * q$$
$$= T \text{ and } T$$
$$= T$$

Example 2:

Let p = improvements total several thousand dollars

Let q = thousands of dollars is an over-improvement

Therefore, the property is over-improved.

$$p = T, q = F$$
from the truth tables:
$$p * q$$
$$T * F$$
$$= F$$

The argument is invalid since there is no information presented to indicate that thousands of dollars is an over-improvement. The invalidity of the argument does not mean the property is not over-improved, but that there is a failure to prove that it is.

Example 4:

Let p = appliances are included in the list price.

Let q = there is an automatic washer and dryer in the utility room.

Therefore, a washer and dryer are included in the list price.

$$p = F, q = T$$
from the truth tables:
$$p * q$$
$$F * T$$
$$= F$$

There is no information to suggest that the washer and dryer are included in the list price, even though the washer and dryer are appliances on the premises, and appliances located on the premises are often included in the list price. There is no information presented to indicate that it is or is not the case that the appliances are included in the price.

CHAPTER 2

RATE OF INTEREST

Interest is payment for the use of borrowed money. The actual amount of money that is borrowed is called the principal amount. The percent of interest charged for the use of principal for one year is called the rate (or rate of interest). The period of time for which interest is paid is called the term of a loan. Interest is expressed as a percentage, the principal is considered the base amount of the loan and the rate percent = the rate of interest * the term of the loan.

Many different methods of computing interest have been developed. Simple interest, compound interest, and compound discount form the basis for most business and finance applications that involve the evaluation or computation of obligations. In calculating interest, the particular method of computation and the variables used in the computation must be understood. The interpretation of the specific terms, method of repayment, and rate will impact the loan.

SIMPLE INTEREST

Simple interest is interest paid on the principal amount only. Simple interest is usually charged on loans that are extended for only a short period of time or on the balance of accounts that are expected to be paid within a short period of time. The term of a simple interest loan is usually a fractional part of the year. The calculation of simple interest involves some commonly used symbols as follows:

P = principal, expressed in dollars

r = annual rate, expressed as a percent

t = term, expressed in years or a fractional part of a year

I = total interest, expressed in dollars

S = amount or sum of the principal and interest, expressed in dollars

The computation for simple interest is, $I = Prt$. Some of the most common problems involving simple interest include finding the percentage, the principal, the rate, and the rate of interest. Formulas for solving such problems are as follows:

$$S = P + I$$
$$\text{Since } I = Prt, \text{ then}$$
$$S = P + Prt = P\,(1 + rt)$$
$$\text{and}$$
$$P = S \div (1 + rt)$$

With these basic formulas, any type of simple interest problem can be solved.

Example:

The interest on $1,750 at 4($\frac{1}{2}$)% for 132 days is calculated as follows:

$$P = \$1,750$$
$$r = 4\ (\tfrac{1}{2})\% = 4.5\%$$
$$t = 132 \text{ days} = 132 \div 365 = 0.36 \text{ yrs}$$
$$I = Prt$$

$$I = \$1,750 * 4.5\% * 0.36 \text{ yrs}$$
$$I = \$28.35$$

The term of a loan is expressed in years or a fraction of a year, but not everyone interprets a year in the same manner. Some computations include a 360-day year and other computations include a 365-day year (or 366 day leap year). For most computations of interest for fractional parts of a year, the amount calculated will not vary significantly whether 12 months, 365 days, or 360 days are used as the basis for computation.

If a year is considered to have 365 days, the interest per day is less than the interest per day if a year is considered to have 360 days since $1/365$ is less than $1/360$. When interest is calculated based on a 360-day year, each month is considered to be 30 days or $1/12$ of a year. The calculated interest is considered ordinary interest. When interest is calculated based on a 365-day (or 366-day leap year), the interest is considered exact interest or accurate interest since its calculation is based on the exact number of days in a year. Interest per day on an exact basis is always less than interest, applied at the same rate, on an ordinary basis. Another form of simple interest that is based on a 360-day year is called banker's interest. In calculating simple interest, there must be some method of determining whether ordinary, exact, or banker's methods are used. The specified rate should also be expressed as some multiple of 100.

Exact Interest and Exact Number of Days

It is customary to count the time between dates using the first or last day of the month or year, but not both. When days in a year are numbered from 1 to 365, the number of days between any given period of time is calculated as the difference between the number of the first date and the number of the last date. This difference is called the exact number of days. The numbered days in a 365-day calendar year can be found in a chart of numbered days, such as the one shown at Appendix 1. The time frame between January 1 and January 31 is actually 30 days, not 31 days, since $31 - 1 = 30$. Likewise, the exact number of days between May 15 and November 4 is calculated as follows:

From the chart of numbered days, it is determined that
May 15 is the 135th day in a 365-day year and
November 4 is the 308th day in a 365-day year.
The difference:
308 days – 135 days
= 173 days, which is the same as above

The table showing numbered days in a year may be used to find the numbered day that corresponds to any particular date. However, if such a chart is not available, the exact time between dates can be calculated as follows:

Term: May 15 through November 4	
Days remaining in May (31 – 15 = 16)	16
Days in June	30
Days in July	31
Days in August	31
Days in September	30
Days in October	31
Days in November	4
Total days:	173

The time interval between dates may span two different calendar years, even though the time frame is less than one year. To calculate the time between dates in different calendar years, find the days remaining in the first year and add it to the days in the second year. If a time frame is specified as November 4 of one year to May 15 of the next year, the number of days is calculated as follows:

November 4 is the 308th day of the year
Days remaining in the first year = 365 – 308 = 57
May 15 is the 135th day of the year
Days in the second year = 135

So, the total number of days in the period = days remaining in the first year + days in the second year
= 57 + 135
= 192 days

Ordinary Interest and the Approximate Number of Days

When each month is considered to have 30 days, the time between dates is calculated as an approximate number of days. This type of count is customarily used in the bond market in determining how long a bond is held and how much interest has accrued on such bonds. This type of ordinary interest may also be referred to as bond interest. Since, in actuality, only one month of the year has less than 30 days and seven months have 31 days, the exact number of days between any two dates is usually greater than the approximate number of days for that same time frame. As such, the calculation of exact number of days favors the party receiving interest payments since interest will be higher.

Banker's Interest

Banker's interest is a form of simple interest where the year is considered to have 360 days, but the actual number of days in a month is counted or exact. Banker's interest does not differ from exact or ordinary interest when a full year is used to compute interest. Differences arise when fractional parts of a year are used.

Banker's interest for one day is equal to $^{1}/_{360}$ of a year's interest whereas exact interest is equal to $^{1}/_{365}$ of a year's interest ($^{1}/_{366}$ for leap years). The relationship between banker's interest and exact interest equates to the proportion:

$$(1 \div 365) \div (1 \div 360) = 360 \div 365 = {}^{72}/_{73}$$

Therefore, exact interest is 72/73 of banker's interest. Exact interest is equal to banker's interest decreased by 1/73 of itself. Conversely, banker's interest is 73/72 of exact interest. Banker's interest is equal to exact interest increased by 1/72 of itself.

The calculation of banker's interest equates to more than exact interest. When a lender draws up a contract, banker's interest is used since it results in greater returns for the lender. The return may only amount to a few cents for an individual borrower, but lenders with thousands of accounts, worth millions of dollars, realize sizable advantages by using the banker's interest method. Governments, which pay interest on billions of dollars for short periods of time, favor the exact method since it results in less interest payments. When a borrower is the party to draw up a contract, the borrower is most likely to use the exact interest method. As such, the exact interest method is customary for municipal securities, U.S. securities, and loans by the Federal Reserve Bank.

The 6% Method

The fact that 6 is a multiple of 360 and 360 is used in calculating ordinary and banker's interests has led to the development of shortcut methods in calculating those interests. The ordinary and banker's interest on $1,000 at 6% for 60 days is calculated as follows:

$$I = Prt$$

$$I = 1000 * \frac{\cancel{6}}{100} * \frac{\cancel{60}}{\cancel{360}}$$

$$= \frac{1000}{100}$$

$$= 10$$

After the possible cancellations are performed, I is equal to 1/100 of the principal amount or $1,000 ÷ 100. As such, the 6% rule specifies that the interest on any amount at 6% for 60 days can be determined by moving the decimal point two places to the left of the principal.

Since 6 days is $^1/_{10}$ of 60 days, it also follows that the interest for 6 days at 6% can be determined by moving the decimal point three places to the left of the principal. Further, if 6 is then divided into that amount, the resulting quotient equates to the interest at 6% for 1 day.

This method may be applied for other rates, such as 3% and 9%, to reduce the complexity in solving problems. These shortcut methods are intended to save time using the principles of fractions and cancellation. There are some circumstances, however, where these short cuts will not save much time. With the advent of calculators and computers, any method of calculating interest can be simplified by automation.

Simple Discount

In simple interest, the amount paid in the future is greater than the amount borrowed or invested. Discount is defined as the difference between the present value of a debt and the value of the debt at its maturity. As such, the future amount (sum S) is greater then the present value (principle P). Debts and their obligation are often expressed in terms of their future value.

Example:

The present value (PV) of what amount, invested at 5%, results in a future value (FV) of $5,000 in one year.

$$r = 5\%$$
$$t = 1 \text{ year}$$
$$S = \$5,000$$

We seek to find the value of P.

$$P = \frac{S}{1 + rt}$$

$$= \frac{5000}{1 + (5\% * 1)}$$

$$= \frac{5000}{1.05}$$

$$= \$4,761.90$$

A 5% return on \$4,761.90 will result in \$5,000 in one year. Likewise, the discount on \$5,000 for one year is \$5,000 − \$4,761.90 = \$238.10. A simple discount is the difference between the present value of a debt and the value of the debt at maturity. The simple interest on P is equal to the simple discount on S.

The simple interest on \$4,761.90 at 5% is \$238.10.

The simple discount on \$5,000 at 5% is \$238.10.

Interest Bearing and Non-Interest Bearing Debts

The present value (or principal) in simple interest assumes that debt does not bear interest. However, it is often necessary to determine the present value of an interest bearing debt. When the discount rate of a note equals the interest rate of the note, the present value is equal to the face amount of the note. However, the two rates are not usually the same. The present value of a debt usually involves one rate, and the debt bears interest at another rate. Thus, two mathematical problems are involved in calculating the present value of an interest bearing debt. The first mathematical problem involves computing the maturity value of the debt using the rate of interest on the note. The second mathematical problem involves computing the present value of the maturity value using a rate of discount. A rate of discount is expressed as either the discount rate or it is designated by the expression "money is worth." The two problems may differ not only in the interest rates applied, but also in the number of periods of time. The steps to solving interest-bearing debt problems are as follows:

Step 1: Determine the date of maturity for the note.

Step 2: Compute the value of the debt at maturity.

Step 3: Determine the discount period.

Step 4: Compute the proceeds (or sum received).

P	→	S
Original value of debt (principal)	Rate of note	Maturity value of debt (sum)
S	→	P
Maturity value of debt at the rate of note	Rate money is worth	Present value of debt at the rate money is worth

Example:

A 90-day note is dated May 18 for $800 at 7%. Money is worth 7(½)%. The note is discounted on July 6. The proceeds are computed as follows:

Step 1:

The date of maturity is 90 days from May 18, which is day 138 of the calendar year. The calendar day corresponding to day 138 + 90 = day 228, which is August 16.

Step 2:

Calculate S = P (1 + rt) where:

P = $800

r = 7%

t = 90/365 = 0.25 days

$$S = P (1 + rt)$$

$$= \$800 * [1 + (7\% * 0.25)]$$
$$= \$800 * [1 + (.07 *0.25)]$$
$$= \$800 * (1 + 0.0175)$$
$$= \$800 * 1.0175$$
$$= \$814 \text{ (the debt at maturity)}$$

Step 3:

The discount period is from July 6 to August 16. July 6 is day 187 of the calendar year and August 16 is day 228. So, day 228 – day 187 = 41 days.

Step 4:

Calculate P = S + (1 + rt), where:
S = $814
r = 7.5%
t = 41/365 = 0.1123287

$$P = \frac{S}{1 + rt}$$
$$= \frac{814}{1 + (.075 * .1123287)}$$
$$= \$814 \div (1 + .0084246)$$
$$= \$814 \div (1.0084246)$$
$$= \$807.20$$

Bank Discounts

Banks do not use true discount. Instead, they figure interest on the maturity value of a debt and deduct the interest from the maturity value of the debt. The amount that is deducted is called a discount. As an example, a bank discounts a $200, 90 day note at 6%. Simple interest is calculated as $I = Prt = \$200 * .06 * {}^{90}/_{365} = \$3.00$.

The amount received by the borrower is $200 – $3 = $197, which is the proceeds or bank proceeds. The $3 deduction from the value of the note is the discount or bank discount. It may be said that the bank discounted the borrower's note or the borrower discounted a note at the bank.

The bank discount calculation is similar to the calculation for simple interest, with the principle replaced by the maturity value of the note and the other variables defined as follows:

S = maturity value of the note

t = number of years, or fractional part of a year between the date of discount and the maturity date of the note

d = the annual bank discount

D = the bank discount

P_b = bank proceeds

D = Sdt

The bank proceeds to the borrower are calculated as:

$$P_b = S - D$$
$$= S - Sdt$$
$$= S (1 - dt)$$
$$\text{and}$$
$$S = P_b \div (1 - dt)$$

Notes discounted by a bank may be either interest bearing or non-interest bearing. In the last example above, a non-interest bearing note was discounted. As such, the maturity value of that note was equivalent to the face value of the note. The period of discount was equal to the time of the note. The proceeds were equal to the difference between the maturity value of the note and the discount.

Example:

The bank discounts a customer's note for 90 days at 6%. The bank proceeds to the customer are $2,800. The face value of the note is:

$$S = P_b \div (1 - dt)$$
$$= \$2,800 \div (1 - .06 * .25)$$
$$= \$2,842.64$$

Bank Discounts on Interest Bearing Notes

With deferred payments, a debtor may agree to pay interest on a loan amount with the terms of the loan specified in a promissory note. The promissory note will specify, among other things, the interest rate to be applied. The face value of the note is equal to the debt, but the value of the debt at maturity is greater than the debt. Rather than wait for the note to mature, a creditor may discount the note at a bank at a specified rate of interest. By acquiring a bank discount, the creditor receives proceeds immediately.

The bank discount of an interest-bearing note requires two computations: a simple interest computation and a bank discount computation. The simple interest computation is necessary to compute the maturity value of a note. This computation is not necessary for non-interest bearing notes. Bank discount computations use the same symbols that are used in simple interest computations, but a bank discount usually involves different values for time and rate than are specified in the original note.

Example:

The banks accepts a 120-day, 6%, $1,000 note from a customer. The customer discounts the note 90 days before the maturity date, and the bank discounts the note at 5%. The bank proceeds to the customer are:

The maturity value of the note is the face value plus simple interest.

$$S = \$1,000 + \$1,000 * .06 * 120/360$$
$$= \$1,020$$

The bank discount on the maturity value is:

$$D = \$1,020 * .05 * 90/360$$
$$= \$12.75$$

The bank proceeds to the customer are:

$$P_b = \$1,020 - \$12.75$$
$$= \$1,007.25$$

Bank discounts are usually computed using the exact number of days. In some instances, the first day of the discount is not included in the time of discount, but the last day of maturity is included. In other instances, both days are included.

Example:

The bank proceeds from the following notes are computed using the steps outlined in the preceding section, Interest Bearing and Non-Interest Bearing Debts.

Face Value of Note	Date of Note	Interest Rate of Note	Term	Date of Bank Discount	Bank Discount Rate	Bank Proceeds
$2,500	4/16	4%	60 days	5/14	5%	$2,505.48
Step 1: 106 + 60 = 166						
Step 2: S = 2,500 * [(1 + (.04 * .1643835)] = 2,500 * 1.0065753 = $2,516.4382						
Step 3: 166 – 134 = 32 days						
Step 4: P = $2,516.4382 ÷ [(1 + (.05 * .0876712] = 2,516.4382 ÷ 1.0043835 = $2,505.48						

Face Value of Note	Date of Note	Interest Rate of Note	Term	Date of Bank Discount	Bank Discount Rate	Bank Proceeds
$1,800	5/14	5%	90 days	5/24	7%	$1,794.15
Step 1: 134 + 90 = 224						
Step 2: S = 1,800 * [(1 + (.05 * .2465753)] = 1,800 * 1.0123287 = $1,822.1916						
Step 3: 224 – 144 = 80 days						
Step 4: P = $1,822.1916 ÷ [(1 + (.07 *.219178)] = 1,822.1916 ÷ 1.0153424 = $1,794.15						

DUE DATE

The average due date, called equated date, is the date on which a series of debts may be equitably discharged by a single payment. This payment must be equal to the face value of the sum of debts. Any past due debts may cause the average due date to be a date that has already passed. However, once the date is known, adjustments may be made from that passed date by adding interest to the amount due. If the payment is to be made earlier than the due date, adjustments are made to discount the amount.

In calculating the average due date, any convenient date may be used as the focal date. However, the earliest due date of all debts is often selected. Since due dates are under consideration, the date of purchase or the date on which an obligation incurred are not taken into consideration. A weighted dollar, known as a dollar day, is used for the calculation. Dollar days are based on the premise that, for any given interest rate, one dollar for one day is just as valuable as another dollar for one day. Debts are converted into dollar days. Payments are also converted into dollar days by multiplying the amount of each debt by the number of days from the due date or focal date. To find the number of days from the focal date, the difference between the dollar days of the debt and the dollar days of payments is divided by the net balance of the debt. The average due date is then calculated by adding or subtracting this calculated number of days from the focal date.

Example:

The following purchases were made on the specified date:

July 30	$750
August 15	$400
August 25	$300

A focal date of July 30 is chosen. The due date is established as July 30, the earliest of all of the purchase dates, and the payments are converted to dollar days.

Due Date	Amount	Days From Focal Date	Dollar Days
July 30	$750	0	0
August 15	$400	16	6,400
August 25	$300	26	7,800
Totals:	$1,450		14,200

Due Date
$$= \$14{,}200 \div \$1{,}450$$
$$= 10$$

The average due date is 10 days beyond the focal date of July 30. Since July has 31 days, there is one day left in the month of July. So the due date is August 9. If payment is made before August 9, the amount may be discounted, and if it is made after August 9, interest may be applied to the amount.

COMPOUND INTEREST

Compound interest is an important part of investment and business decisions. When money is borrowed for a short period of time, the lender anticipates receiving the amount of the loan plus interest at the maturity of the loan. At the time of payment, the lender has the option of re-lending, investing, or spending the principal amount, as well as any income received as interest on the principal. If the lender chooses to re-lend the sum of principal and interest for another period, the lender, in effect, receives interest on the original principle and its interest.

Example 1:

A $1,000 loan is made at 6% interest for 6 months, and the lender receives $1,030 when the loan is paid.

107

$I = Prt$, where $P = \$1,000$, $r = 6\% = .06\%$, and $t = 6$ months $= 6 \div 12$
yrs $= 0.5$ yrs
$I = \$1,000 * 0.6 * 0.5 = \$30.00$
The sum: $S = IP = \$1,000 + \$30$
$= \$1,030$

If the lender decides to re-lend the sum to another borrower at 6 % for 6 months, the lender will receive $1,060.90 when this new loan is repaid.

$I = Prt$, where $P = \$1,030$, $r = 6\% = .06\%$, and $t = 6$ months $= 6 \div 12$
yrs $= 0.5$ yrs
$I = \$1,030 * 0.6 * 0.5 = \$30.90$
The sum: $S = IP = \$1,030 + \$30.90$
$= \$1,060.90$

In the two 6 month periods, the lender receives $30 + $30.90 = $60.90 in interest. If, instead, the lender had loaned $1,000 at 6% for 1 year, he would receive only $60 in interest at maturity. The lender receives less return for the longer-term loan than the two short-term loans. To make the two loan scenarios equitable, the lender would need to make the long-term loan at a higher interest rate or require that interest be paid periodically. In our example, the lender would need to raise the interest rate on the longer term loan to 6.09% to receive the same $1,060.90 return that was received from the two short term loans or require payment at the end of the first 6-month period and then re-loan or invest the return at the same rate.

Compound interest is interest received on a principal amount, which is increased periodically by interest incurred during the period. Compound interest differs from simple interest since the principal does not remain constant, but varies during the term of a loan. Compound interest essentially allows interest to be earned on interest. Symbols used in calculating compound interest are as follows:

P = principal or present value. The initial amount lent, borrowed, or invested, expressed in dollars.

i = interest rate per period, expressed as a percent. This rate may be stated as an annual rate or the rate for any given period.

n = number of interest periods, expressed as an integer.

I = total interest, expressed in dollars.

S = compound amount or sum of the compounded principal and interest, expressed in dollars.

m = frequency of conversion, expressed as an integer.

j = nominal (annual) interest rate, expressed as a percent.

Compound vs. Simple Interest

When interest is paid or added to the principal once per year, the interest is considered compounded or converted annually. However, interest may also be converted at other regular periods, such as monthly, quarterly, or semiannually. The number of times for which interest is converted per year is called the frequency of conversion. The frequency of conversion is represented by the symbol m. If interest is converted quarterly, m = 4 and the conversion period is 4 months.

In simple interest calculations, the interest rate is represented by r and it always signifies an annual rate. When interest rates are calculated annually, the rate is referred to as a nominal interest rate (or nominal rate). In calculating compound interest, a rate per conversion period, also called a periodic rate, is used. The symbol used for periodic rate is i. Periodic rate is calculated by dividing the nominal rate by the frequency of conversion. Only when interest is compounded annually does the periodic rate equal the nominal rate. The nominal interest rate is often represented by the symbol j. Hence $i = j \div m$.

In compound interest, the actual rate of increase during the year is called the effective rate. If the frequency of conversion is greater than one, the effective rate of interest will always exceed the nominal rate of interest. If interest is converted annually, the effective rate and nominal rate are equal. When a frequency of conversion is not stated, it is assumed to be annual.

In simple interest calculations, time is represented by t and it signifies years or the fractional part of a year. Since interest is not always converted annually in compound interest, time is measured by the number of conversion periods in a year rather than years or fractional parts of years. In the computation of compound interest, the rate per period and number of periods must be known. The number of periods is found by multiplying the time in years by the frequency of conversion. Hence, $n = t * m$. If compound interest is used to compute the interest on $5,000 for 10 years at 6% interest converted quarterly, the value of n is $10 * 4 = 40$, not 4. The frequency of conversion over the 10-year period is 4. The conversion period is 3 months, and the interest per period is $6\% \div 4 = 1.68\%$ (effective).

Determining the Compound Sum

In compound interest calculations, the sum of principal and interest, S $= P(1 + i)$. As such, the sum at the end of the first period is defined as:

$$S = P(1 + i)$$

At the end of the second period, the amount is calculated as the sum at the end of the first period times $(1 + i)$.

$$S_2 = S + (1 + i)$$

$$S_2 = P (1 + i) + (1 + i)$$
$$S_2 = P (1 + i)^2$$

At the end of the third quarter, the sum is calculated as:

$$S_3 = S_2 + (1 + i)$$
$$S_3 = P (1 + i)^2 + (1 + i)$$
$$S_3 = P (1 + i)^3$$

Since n represents the number of periods, the sum at the end of any period could be expressed as:

$$S = P (1 + i)^n$$

Example 1:

If the principal P = $2,000, n = 5 periods, and i = 2($\frac{1}{2}$)% = 2.5%, the accumulated sum is calculated as follows:

$$S = P (1 + i)^n$$
$$S = \$2,000 (1 + 2.5)^5$$
$$S = \$2,000 (1.025)^5$$
$$= \$2,262.82$$

Example 2:

The interest on $326.40 compounded semiannually at 6% for 10 years is calculated as follows:

The principal: P = $326.40

The number of periods: n = 2 * 10 = 20

The frequency of conversion: m = 2

The nominal rate of interest: j = 6 %

The periodic rate of interest: i = j ÷ m = 6% ÷ 2 = 3%

$$S = P (1 + i)^n$$

$$= \$326.40 * (1 + 3\%)^{20}$$
$$= \$326.40 * (1 + .03)^{20}$$
$$= \$326.40 * (1.03)^{20}$$
$$= \$326.40 * 1.806111235$$
$$= \$589.51$$

This amount includes both the original principal and the compounded interest over the 10-year time frame. In order to determine only the compound interest amount, the original principal amount must be subtracted from this sum. So, the compound interest amount is:

$$\$589.51 - \$326.40 = \$263.11$$

Compound Interest Tables

Computations of compound interest may be simplified with the use of a compound interest table, such as that included in the table at Appendix 4, or some method of digital computation. Compound interest tables are constructed to provide a compound amount, given the rate per period and nominal interest rate. The table is constructed such that compound interest amounts fall under the column headings $(1+i)^n$. The table is constructed as follows:

- Each section of the table provides data for various rates of interest, for example $i = \frac{1}{4}\%$.

- The column labeled n lists the number of periods.

- The column labeled $(1 + i)^n$, which is the formula for a compound sum with principal, P = zero, contains tabular data for the amount of one. The amount of one is defined as how $1 dollar will grow at compound interest.

The values in the table are shown to eight decimal places. If these values are rounded to include the same number of decimal places as there are significant places (dollars and cents) in the multiplier, answers correct to the nearest cent can be obtained for amounts up to $100,000.00. However, in all likelihood, a calculator will be used for these types of computations, and the results provided by such electronic devices are often sufficient for most applications, even though the result may or may not offer the same accuracy.

To find a compound amount, the section corresponding to the particular rate per period is located. The tabular value, which corresponds to the number of periods n, is then located. The tabular value is then multiplied by the principal amount P.

Example 1:

We compute the compound sum for the previous example using the compound interest table for $i = 3\%$. We find the tabular value that corresponds to $n = 20$ is 1.8061112347. If we multiply this value by the principal $P = \$3{,}276.40$, we have the sum of $589.51, as before.

Example 2:

An investor borrows $10,000 at 9% with interest to be compounded and paid monthly. The investor fails to make the monthly payments on interest. Instead, the principal and interest continue to be compounded monthly and must be paid at the end of the year. The amount due at the end of the year is calculated as follows:

$$P = \$10{,}000$$
$$i = 9\% \div 12 = 0.75\%$$
$$n = 12$$
$$S = P\,(1 + i)^n$$
$$= \$10{,}000 * (1 + 0.75\%)^{12}$$
$$= \$10{,}000 * (1 + .0075)^{12}$$
$$= \$10{,}000 * (1.0075)^{12}$$

$$= \$10{,}000 * 1.093806898$$
$$= \$10,938.07$$

Example 3:

We compute the compound sum for the previous example using the compound interest table for $i = {}^{3}/_{4}\%$. We find the tabular value that corresponds to $n = 12$ is 1.0938068977. If we multiply this value by the principal $P = \$10{,}000$, we have the sum of $\$10{,}938.07$, as before.

Determining the Number of Periods

In problems involving compound interest, it may be necessary to determine the periodic rate or number of periods rather than the amount of accumulated interest. Since $S = P(1 + i)^n$, the value of n may be found using logarithms. Given that $\log(a * b) = \log a + \log b$ and the $\log a^b = b \log a$, the number of periods is calculated as follows:

$$\log S = \log[P(1 + i)^n]$$
$$\log S = \log P + \log(1 + i)^n$$
$$\log S = \log P + [n * \log(1 + i)]$$
$$\text{and}$$
$$n = \frac{\log S - \log P}{\log(1 + i)}$$

A table of logarithms could be used to solve this equation, but that would require a very laborious process, which will not be discussed here. A simpler method of finding the solution is to make use of a scientific calculator.

Example:

The time required for any amount of money to double itself at 5% interest compounded annually is calculated as follows:

$S = 2 * P$
$i = 5\%$ per period
$n = 1$ year

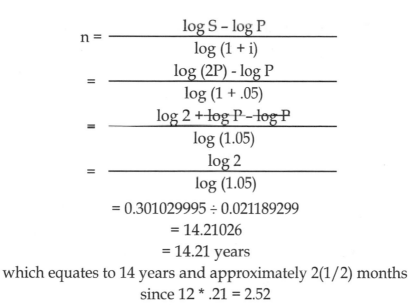

$$n = \frac{\log S - \log P}{\log (1 + i)}$$

$$= \frac{\log (2P) - \log P}{\log (1 + .05)}$$

$$= \frac{\log 2 + \cancel{\log P} - \cancel{\log P}}{\log (1.05)}$$

$$= \frac{\log 2}{\log (1.05)}$$

$$= 0.301029995 \div 0.021189299$$
$$= 14.21026$$
$$= 14.21 \text{ years}$$

which equates to 14 years and approximately 2(1/2) months
since 12 * .21 = 2.52

Determining the Periodic Rate

When making decisions regarding investment opportunities, most investors will consider the rate of interest to be paid or received. A decision may be made based on the compound amount as computed at the end of a period. This decision, however, is complicated when the sums, number of periods, and frequency of conversion differ among the investment opportunities. To simplify such comparisons, investors may change all rates under consideration to a comparable basis. This is achieved by computing an effective interest rate, which is a measure of the actual rate of increase during a one-year period.

If interest is converted more than once per year, an effective rate should be determined. The effective rate is determined by subtracting 1 from the sum $(1 + i)$ for the number of periods specified in the frequency of conversion.

Example:

The effective rate that is equivalent to 4% converted quarterly is computed as follows:

The frequency of conversion: m = 4
The periodic interest: i = 4% ÷ 4 =1%

So,
$$(1 + i)^n - 1$$
$$= (1 + 1\%)^4 - 1$$
$$= (1.01)^4 - 1$$
$$= 1.040660401 - 1$$
$$= 0.0406$$
$$= 4.1\%$$

Non-Integral Conversion Periods

Conversion periods in compound interest do not necessarily have to be integral values. Often times when interest is compounded, the conversion period may be specified as some number of years and/or months.

Example:

The amount on $3,265 compounded semiannually for 20 years and 4 months at 8% is computed as follows:

P = $3,265
r = 8% and i = 4% per period
n = 40(4/6) = 40(2/3)

$$S = P (1 + i)^n$$
$$= \$3{,}265 * (1 + 4\%)^{122/3}$$
$$= \$3{,}265 * (1.04)^{40.67}$$
$$= \$3{,}265 * 4.928853494$$
$$= \$16{,}092.70666$$
$$= \$16{,}092.71$$

If the table of compound interest is used, the solution involves determining the compound interest for the integral number of periods and then calculating and adding a simple interest computation on this amount for the fractional part of the period.

Using the same example, the tabular value of compound interest for 40 periods is 4.80102063 and the sum = 4.80102063 * $3,265 = $15,675.33.

The simple interest on this amount for 4/12 years is:

$$I = Prt$$
$$= \$15{,}675.33 * .08 * {}^{1}/_{3}$$
$$= \$418.0088$$
$$= \$418.01$$
$$\$15{,}675.33 + \$418.01 = \$16{,}093.34$$

This is the same as above with some error due to rounding.

Effect of Frequency Conversion on Effective Rates

In compound interest, a periodic rate is used as the basis for computations. The more frequent the number of conversions, the sooner interest is paid on accrued interest. As such, the effective rate of interest is increased as the frequency of conversion is increased. However, as the number of conversions is increased, only a progressively smaller increase in the effective rate is achieved.

Example:

A nominal rate of 6% compounded at the following frequencies produces the following effective rates:

6% Compounded	Number of Conversions Per Year	Effective Rate of Interest
Annually	1	6%

Semiannually	2	6.09%
Quarterly	4	6.13636%
Monthly	12	6.16778%
Weekly	52	6.17998%
Daily	365	6.18313%
Continuously	Infinity	6.18365%

These values indicate that little gain is achieved by increasing the frequency of conversion beyond one month. Though the concept of continuous compounding has no real mathematical application in finance, real estate, or investments, it is presented here for clarity to indicate the limit of annual growth. It should be noted that continuous compounding does have application in nature as a rate of growth.

Discounts in Compound Interest

Compound interest is used to determine the future value of a present sum. It also may be used to determine the present value of a future sum. Even though present value is thought to indicate the value now and future value is thought to indicate a value sometime in the future, mathematically, it does not matter whether present value is used to indicate now, some time in the past, or some time in the future. Likewise, it does not matter whether future value is used to indicate now, some time in the past, or some time in the future. It is relationship between any two chosen dates that is mathematically significant.

The difference between an amount S and principal P compounded at 9% for 5 years is the same regardless of whether either date is used to represent now, the past, or the future.

$$\text{If } S = P (1 + i)^n$$
$$\text{then}$$
$$P = S \div (1 + i)^n$$

and
$$P = S * (1 + i)^{-n}$$

To find the present value of a future sum, the future value must be discounted. The difference between the future value and the present value is called the compound discount. The term $(1 + i)^n$ is called the discount factor. The formula for present value is derived from the formula for compound amount, with all symbols having the same meaning.

P = principle, which represents the value of an obligation at some date

S = sum, which represents the amount of that obligation, n periods in the future

P		S
(value now)	n periods	(value in n periods)

The difference between P and S can be thought of as either

- The compound interest on P in n periods or

- The discount, at the compound interest rate, on S

The present value of a non-interest bearing note is found by computing the compound amount until maturity. However, the present value of an interest-bearing note requires a calculation of the compound amount and a calculation of the discount on the maturity value of the note.

Example 1:
A note for $3,000 is due in 4 years with 5% interest. The current interest rate charged on similar types of loans is 4%. The present value of the note is calculated as follows:

The value of the note at maturity is calculated as $S = P (1 + i)^n$ where:

$P = \$3,000 \qquad i = .05 \qquad n = 4$

$$S = \$3,000 \ (1 + .05)^4$$
$$= 3000 * 1.21550625$$
$$= \$3,646.52$$

The present value of \$3,646.52 due in 4 years at 4% is calculated as P = S ÷ (1 + i)^n where:

S = 3,646.52
i = .04
n = 4

$$P = S \div (1 + i)^n$$
$$= 3,646.52 \div (1 + .04)^4$$
$$= 3,646.52 \div 1.16985856$$
$$= \$3,117.06$$

The present value of the note is \$3,117.06.

The discount applied to the note is the difference between the value of the note at maturity and the present value of the note. The discount is \$3,646.52 – \$3,117.06 = \$529.46.

Example 2:

The 2-year discount on \$5,000 at 4% is determined for each of the following types of discount:

Simple Discount	$P = S \div (1 + rt)$ = \$5,000 ÷ [1 + (.04 * 2)] = \$5,000 ÷ 1.08 = \$4,629.62 Discount = \$5,000 - \$4,629.62 = \$370.37
Compound Discount	$P = S \div (1 + i)^n$ = \$5,000 ÷ (1 .08)$^{-2}$ = \$4,622.78 Discount = \$5,000 – \$4,622.78 = \$377.22

Bank Discount	$P_b = S * (1 - dt)$ $= \$5,000 * [1 - (.04 * 2)]$ $= \$4,600$ Discount $= \$5,000 - \$4,600$ $= \$400$
Compound Discount Converted Semiannually	$P = S \div (1 + i)^n$ $= \$5,000 \div (1.02)^{-4}$ $= \$4,619.23$ Discount $= \$5,000 - \$4,619.23$ $= \$380.77$

VALUE OF AN OBLIGATION

Many times it will be necessary to determine the value of an obligation either before or after a specified payment date. The value of a non-interest bearing amount of $1,000 compounded at 6% annually and due in the year 2010 may be represented as follows:

YEAR	AMOUNT	
2000	$\$1,000 * (1 + 6\%)^{-10}$	$558.39
2005	$\$1,000 * (1 + 6)^{-3}$	$-747.26
2009	$\$1,000 * (1 + 6\%)^{-1}$	$943.40
2010	$1,000	$1,000
2011	$\$1,000 * (1 + 6\%)$	$-1,060.00
2015	$\$1,000 * 1 + 6\%)^{+5}$	$-1,338.23
2020	$\$1,000 * 1 + 6\%)^{+10}$	$1,790.85

The table shows that $1,000 due in 2010 is worth only $558.39 ten years earlier and $1,790.85 ten years in the future.

To find the value of an amount before the due date, the discount factor, $(1 + i)^n$, is used to discount the amount for the particular amount of time. To find the value of an amount after the due date, the compound interest must be determined.

Example:

An investor owes a debt of $5,000, which is due in 4 years. The investor expects to sell two homes, the first of which is expected to sell in 2 years with a profit of $2,500. This amount will be used to reduce the $5,000 debt. Money is worth 5%. The balance of the debt at the end of the fourth year is calculated as follows:

The value of $2,500 compounded at 5% for 2 years is:

$$S = \$2,500 \, (1 + .05)^2$$
$$= \$2,500 * 1.1025$$
$$= \$2,756.25$$

The original $5,000 debt will be reduced by $2,756.25, leaving a balance of $2,243.75 at the end of the fourth year.

EQUATION OF PAYMENT

Many times it is necessary to find one amount that is equivalent to two or more obligations. For example, two separate notes are owned. One note is due in two years and the other note is due in five years. Equation of payment is used to determine a sum of money that is equivalent to the two separate obligations that are due at different times. In compound interest, it may be necessary to commute one set of obligations into another set. In other words, it may be necessary to substitute one set of obligations to be paid in one manner for another set of obligations to be paid in a different manner. The old set of obligations is determined and a new set of obligations is established as equivalent to the old set of obligations on a given date. This date is the focal date in compound interest. If one set of obligations is equivalent to another set of obligations on a given date, the obligations remain equivalent on any other date. The focal date is usually chosen as the date on which payment is made, but may be any chosen date.

The steps to solving equation of payment problems at compound interest are as follows:

Step 1: Select the date of the first unknown payment as the focal date.

Step 2: Compute the equivalent value of each of the original sets of obligations on the focal date.

Step 3: Compute the equivalent value of each new obligation on the focal date.

Step 4: Equate the sum of the two sets of equivalent values.

Step 5: Solve the algebraic equation for the value of the unknown payment or for each of the unknown payments.

Example 1:

We want to commute the debts of $500 due in 2 years and $1,000 due in 3 years to two equal payments due in 2 and 3 years, respectively. Money is worth 5%, annually.

Step 1: The focal point is chosen as 2 years.

Step 2: The original $500 debt is already established at the focal date.

The original $1,000 debt must be commuted to the focal date. The 3-year debt is discounted for one year:

$$S = \$1,000 * (1 + .05)^{-1}$$
$$= \$1,000 * .952380952$$
$$= \$952.3809524$$

Step 3: The new obligations require that x be paid in 2 years and x be paid in 3 years. The second payment of x must be commuted to the focal date. As such, the second payment of x must be discounted by 1 year.

Step 4: The sum of the new obligations on the focal date must be equal to the sum of the old obligations on the focal date. As such:

$$500 + \$1{,}000 * (1 + .05)^{-1} = x + x (1 + .05)^{-1}$$
$$500 + 952.3809524 = x + (x * 0.952380952)$$
$$1.952380952 * x = 1{,}452.380952$$
$$x = \$743.90$$

Two payments of \$743.90 will be made in years 2 and 3, respectively.

Example 2:

An investor has debt totaling \$28,000 that is distributed as follows:

A \$4,000 note at 5% that is 1 year past due.

A 3-year, \$10,000 note at 5% that is due in 1 year.

A \$14,000 non-interest bearing note that is due in 5 years.

The investor would like to commute these debts such that the \$10,000 note is due in 2 years and the two other non-interest bearing notes for the same amount are due in 4 and 6 years. Money is worth 4(½)% per year. The face value of the two notes is calculated as follows:

Step 1: The focal point is chosen as 4 years.

Step 2: (a) The \$4,000 note is past due by 1 year and the present value is:

$$S = P (1 + i)^n$$
$$= \$4{,}000 (1 + 5\%)^1$$

$$= \$4{,}000 * 1.05$$
$$= \$4{,}200$$

$4{,}200 commuted to the focal date of 4 years:

$$S = P\,(1 + i)^n$$
$$= \$4{,}200\,(1 + 4.5\%)^4$$
$$= \$4{,}200 * 1.192518601$$
$$= \$5{,}008.578123$$
$$= \$5{,}008.58$$

(b) The \$10,000 note has been compounded for 3 years at 5(1/2)% and the present value is:

$$S = P\,(1 + i)^n$$
$$= \$10{,}000\,(1 + 5.5\%)^3$$
$$= \$10{,}000 * 1.17241375$$
$$= \$11{,}742.41375$$
$$= \$11{,}742.41$$

$11{,}742.41, commuted to the focal date, which is in 3 years:

$$S = P\,(1 + i)^n$$
$$= \$11{,}742.41\,(1 + 4.5\%)^3$$
$$= \$11{,}742.41 * 1.141166125$$
$$= \$13{,}400.04052$$
$$= \$13{,}400.04$$

(c) The \$14,000 note is due in 5 years and is discounted for 1 year to commute it to the focal date:

$$S = P\,(1 + i)^n$$
$$= \$14{,}000\,(1 + 4.5\%)^{-1}$$
$$= \$14{,}000 * 0.956937799$$
$$= \$13{,}397.12919$$
$$= \$13{,}397.13$$

Step 3: The new obligations on the focal date are x to be paid in 4 years and x to be paid in 6 years.

(a) The new obligations require that the $1,000 note be due in 2 years:

$$S = P (1 + i)^n$$
$$= \$10,000 (1 + 4.5\%)^2$$
$$= \$10,000 * 1.092025$$
$$= \$10,920.25$$

(b) x is to be paid in 4 years

(c) x is to be paid in 6 years. As such, the second payment of x must be discounted by 2 years:

$$x (1 + 4.5\%)^{-2}$$
$$= x * 0.915729951$$

Step 4: The sum of the new obligations on the focal date must be equal to the sum of the old obligations on the focal date. As such:

$$\$4,200 (1 + 4.5\%)^4 + \$11,742.41 (1 + 4.5\%)^3 + \$14,000 (1 + 4.5\%)^{-1} =$$
$$\$10,000 (1 + 4.5\%)^2 + x + x (1 + 4.5\%)^{-2}$$
$$\$5,008.58 + \$13,400.04 + \$13,397.13 = \$10,920.25 + x + 0.915729951x$$
$$\$20,885.5 = 1.915729951x$$
$$x = 10,902.11$$

Making a payment of $10,000 in 2 years, a payment of $10,902.11 in 4 years, and a final payment of $10,902.11 in 6 years will pay the three original obligations.

INVESTMENT MATHEMATICS

EQUATION OF VALUE

Often it is necessary to make comparisons between two or more sums of money that are due at different times and may bear interest. Such values cannot be compared unless one of the values is discounted to or accumulated to the date for which the other is due. The date selected for such a comparison is known as the focal date or equation of value. The equation used to relate two or more sums of money on a focal date is called an equation of value.

The present value of money due in the future is dependent on the time lapse before the amount is due and the rate of interest used in determining the present value. If money is worth 6%, any amount that exists now will be worth its face value plus 6% in the future. This precludes that a person who places a worth of 6% on x = $1,000 dollars is just as likely to accept y = $943.40 dollars today as $1,000 in the future. The value x is known as the future value (FV) and the value y is known as present value (PV). The calculation of present value is:

$$PV = \frac{FV}{1 + rt}$$

Where t = 1 year

PV = $1,000 ÷ 1 + (6% * 1)

$$PV = \$1,000 \div (1 + .06)$$
$$PV = \$1,000 \div (1\ .06)$$
$$PV = \$943.40$$

An examination of this formula for present value shows that it is the same as that used to calculate principle in simple interest calculations. In simple interest calculations, $P = S + (1 + rt)$. The simple interest principle is equivalent to present value. Likewise, simple interest sum is equivalent to future value, and the calculation for future value is as follows:

$$FV = PV\ (1 + rt)$$

COST OF MONEY

The cost of borrowing money is expressed in terms of the interest rate assessed on a loan and the portion of a loan payment that is the lender's charge for borrowing the money. Changes in the interest rates that lenders charge to borrow money against an income producing property have a direct effect on the value of the property. An income producing property provides a stream of income, which is generated by the operation of that property, independent of external factors that allow one to hold title and rights to the property or prolong the life of the property, such as financing, taxes, and capital improvements. When an investor purchases income-producing property, the investor is purchasing the income stream associated with that property.

The income capitalization method of appraisals provides that income streams be converted into a single capital value. As such, any reduction in the income stream reduces the capital value. Further, the cost of money borrowed for the property negatively impacts the income stream and subsequently reduces the capital value. The higher the interest rate on borrowed money, the greater the amount one must pay to borrow money. A change in rates may have only a minimal impact on the investment amount needed for smaller loans of thousands of dollars, but it will have a significant impact on larger loans of millions of dollars.

Example:

The monthly payment for a loan of $2,525,000 with a term of 30 years is calculated as follows for the various interest rates:

5.25%	5.75%	6.25%	6.75%	7.25%
$13,943.14	$14,735.21	$15,546.86	$16,377.1	$17,224.95

The monthly payment at 7.25% is 17,224.95. If the interest rate is reduced by 0.5%, the monthly payment is reduced to $16,377.1. The difference in payment is $847.85 per month or $10,174.20 over one year.

This reduction in the interest rate provides the investor with a savings of $10,174.20 over a one-year period, and as such, the income stream of the property increases by the same amount. To capitalize the value of the increased income stream, the cash flow is converted to a single capital value. A value of 10% is assumed for the capitalization rate, and the present value of the income stream is calculated as follows:

$$PV \text{ (income stream)}$$
$$= \text{income} \div \text{capitalization rate}$$
$$= \$10,174.20 \div .10$$
$$= \$1,017.42$$

The increased income stream is capitalized to a single capital value of $1,017.42 as a direct result of the reduction of the cost to borrow money for the property. The value of the property does not change since financing has no effect on the net operating income (NOI). Only the return on investment is increased as a result of the additional cash flow.

Amortization Period

The amortization period of a loan is the length of time used to calculate loan payments over the term of the loan. A loan is fully amortized if it is repaid. An amortization schedule is a listing of scheduled payments over the term of the loan. It shows the portion of payment to be applied to the principal and the portion of payment to be applied to interest. The amortization schedule provides the investor with an overview of the payment necessary to reduce the balance of the loan at any given point. The longer the term of the loan, the lower the periodic payments. Likewise, the shorter the term of the loan, the higher the periodic payment amounts.

It is common for mortgage lenders to extend mortgage loans for terms of 15 or 30 years. The difference in payments may be significant depending on the interest rate charged. The investor must decide which term of the loan is most suitable for his or her situation. It is recommended that investors engage in the longer-term loan because it provides greater flexibility in payment. The investor could always apply more payment to the longer-term loan than is required, without an obligation to do so. Also, cash out-flows from income property are minimized by the longer term, smaller payment amount. Many investors may prefer shorter-term loans so that they may pay off any debt on the property as soon as possible and it is sooner, rather than later, that they begin to receive a higher return from the property. However, this may still be accomplished with a longer-term loan by paying more than the required amount. Further, the lower payment amount required of the longer-term loan provides the investor with a safety net if unexpected vacancies or uncollectible rents occur. The trade off in prepaying the loan amount is that the additional principal applied to the loan balance reduces the monthly cash flow from the property.

Borrowed Money

The amount of money borrowed to finance an investment or the total loan amount has an inverse relationship to the down payment for the loan. As the total loan amount increases, the less is required for a down payment, and as the total loan amount decreases, the more is required for a down payment. For loans with similar terms, the more money borrowed, the greater the monthly payment amount and the less money borrowed, the less the monthly payment amount. It may seem logical to conclude that it is best to make as large a down payment as possible to reduce the monthly payment amount and increase the cash flow amount. However, when leverage is considered, this logic fails. Leverage is the concept of using other people's money, and this concept is well accepted and encouraged in real estate investment. Leverage precludes that the greater the percentage of money borrowed, the greater the return on equity. As such, monthly payment amounts may be greater due to leverage, but it allows the investor to maintain his or her own money and make use of other people's money, primarily the lender's money. By increasing the amount of borrowed money and decreasing the amount of out of pocket investment, an investor earns a higher rate of return on the investment.

As an example, Investor A and Investor B purchase properties for the same amount. They both leverage their investments and borrow at the same rate of interest for the same term of payment. However, Investor A leverages 75% of the purchase price and makes a down payment for the remaining 25% of the purchase price. Investor B, on the other hand, leverages 90% of the purchase price and pays only a 10% down payment. As such, the monthly payment amount on Investor A's loan is less than that of Investor B since Investor B borrowed more money. Furthermore, Investor A will have a larger monthly cash flow than Investor B. If monthly cash flow were the only basis for comparison, it would seem that Investor A made the wisest investment decision. However, if the amount of leverage is taken into consideration and the ratios of net income ROI, cash ROI, and total ROI are computed, Investor A's decision may not be so wise.

Example:

Investor A and Investor B purchase properties for the same price, but Investor A leverages 75% of the purchase price while Investor B leverages 90% of the purchase price. Investor A spends $17,263 of the income from the property to service the debt on the property and Investor B spends $20,845 to service the debt on his property. So, Investor A enjoys a monthly cash flow, $20,854 – $17,263 = $3,591 more than Investor B. The returns on investment are computed and provide the following results:

	Investor A	Investor B
Net income ROI	5.62	4.43
Cash ROI	14.26	22.01
Total ROI	18.45	36.42

When the ratios of return on investment are computed it is found that Investor A has a total return on his cash investment of 18.45% and Investor B has a total return on his cash investment of 36.42%, which is more than double that of Investor A. Investor B increased the amount of funds borrowed (or leveraged) and decreased the amount of funds invested as compared to Investor A. As such, Investor B receives a higher rate of return even though his monthly cash flow is less and his debt is more.

Loan Duration

There is no one method of determining the best duration for the repayment of a loan. The duration of a loan should be chosen such that it best suits the needs and goals of the investor. Investors must take into consideration the additional fees charged by lenders and how those fees affect the overall cost of a loan and the investment. Investors should also determine whether a particular lender imposes prepayment penalties for the overpayment of a loan before securing the loan.

Loan duration is the life of a loan, also called the term of the loan. Loan duration of 15 years implies that the loan will be paid in full or renewed at the end of the 15-year period. Loan duration is not to be confused with an amortization schedule. Amortization is used in calculating the amount of payment, whereas loan duration is the length of time for which the loan will exist. A loan with duration of 10 years may have payments according to a 15- or 30-year amortization schedule. If the loan payments are not sufficient to pay off the loan during the 10-year term of the loan, any outstanding balance will be due in full at the end of the 10-year period unless the lender decides to extend or renew the loan.

It is the responsibility of the investor to understand the terms of any acquired loan and to be sure that his or her interpretation of the terms is the same as that of the lender. The terms specified for a particular loan will affect the financing of real estate, and the most appropriate term is a function of how long the investment is expected to be held. In general, an investor should choose a loan with terms that meet or exceed the expected life of the investment so that no further financing will be necessary during the life of the investment. The term of any chosen loan should match the full amortization period of the loan, which is typically 30 years. If a property is to be held for a short period of time, there are disadvantages to long-term financing. If, for example, a property is purchased for the purpose of rehabbing it within a year and then selling it, the investor may only want to secure a short-term loan. Short-term loans typically offer lower interest rates simply because lenders are more capable of predicting interest rates over short time frames than they are over long time frames.

Investors should attempt to lock into interest rates that are lowest during the initial financing. Interest rates have a tendency to fluctuate, and if rates are reduced, the investor can always refinance the loan. However, if prepayment penalties are assessed against the loan, refinancing may not be a viable option. An appropriately chosen loan should not be adversely affected by an increase in market interest rates.

Lender Fees

The financing of a property requires expenses other than the interest incurred on the loan. Lender fees are loan fees as assessed by the lender. Lender fees are assessed under various names such as application fees, loan origination fees, underwriting fees, mortgage broker fees, points, and many others. It is advantageous to the investor to request a listing of all fees assessed by both the lender and the mortgage broker, if applicable. The law requires all lenders and real estate brokers to provide disclosure of all costs that will be required for the purchase of property. Specifically, the federal real estate Settlement Procedures Act requires that lenders provide borrowers with a good faith estimate of all reasonable and customary fees due at closing. The law further requires that the estimate be provided within three days of signing a loan application. However, laws do not govern the meaning of terms used in such disclosures. Also, the law requires an estimate, not the actual costs. Even after such disclosure is provided, additional charges have been known to be included in settlement statements just prior to closing. This is due primarily to disconnect between the broker and the lender. Brokers indicate that they are not always aware of the fee structure used by lenders, particularly those lenders they have not used in the past.

A good faith estimate should provide mortgage fees, which are termed settlement costs. These costs vary from lender to lender and are assessed to cover the numerous expenses associated with financing a loan. The estimate may also include fees assessed by parties other than the lender who have an interest in the loan or loan process. A good faith estimate should be received before providing signage to a loan. A good faith estimate may be requested from several lenders for comparison purposes before settling on any one particular loan.

Lenders may assess a loan application fee as part of the application process. These types of application fees may range from zero dollars to as much as $500 on a single family residential property or as much as $500 to $5,000 on a multifamily residential property or a commercial property. Such application fees are nonrefundable and advertised to offset administrative costs and the cost of acquiring credit reports. However, the fees have been instrumental in assisting the lender with filtering out applicants that are not likely to qualify for a loan. If an applicant has a bad credit history, for example, that applicant may be less willing to pay a $500, un-refundable application if he or she knows they are unlikely to qualify for a loan. Lenders that charge application fees may have fewer applicants, but it also has the effect of providing those lenders with more quality applicants. Another reason that lenders justify application fees is to cover the charge of processing applicants who do not qualify for a loan. In this and some other instances, application fees are negotiable. An applicant, who has good credit and presents a good credit risk, may ask that the fee be waived. The lender is likely to provide a favorable response, but in many instances, the fee will still be charged and refunded as a credit during closing. This protects the lender from the risk of having the applicant switch to another lender.

Loan origination fees are usually the equivalent of 1% of the loan amount or 1 point. This cost is justified as the expense to make a loan once the loan is approved. In making a loan, legal documents are crated and processed, funds are secured, and all paperwork is properly recorded. Some lenders may waive the origination fee, while others may roll the fee amount over into the interest rate. This type of rollover has the effect of increasing the interest rate by as much as 25 basis points, which is the equivalent of $1/_4$ of a point.

Underwriting fees are justified as the expense to have underwriters actually underwrite the loan.

Mortgage broker fees are the largest source of income for mortgage brokers. Since brokers are not lenders, they do not earn any part of the interest charged on loans that they are responsible to place. Mortgage brokers are similar to real estate brokers in that they only earn compensation as a percentage of what they are able to sell. Mortgage brokers, however, are compensated with points, rather than commission. Brokers often receive an amount in the range of 1 to 2% of the loan amount. The borrower's creditworthiness, the size of the loan, and back-end fees from the lender are all factored into the mortgage broker's fee. Back-end fees are compensation paid to mortgage brokers when the broker's compensation would otherwise be less than the typical rate charged. As an example, the base rate charged by a lender is 6.25% with zero points. The lender is likely to compensate the broker with a back-end fee of 1% of the loan amount. If the broker is able to sell the same loan at 6.5%, the broker is likely to increase the back-end fee. The broker may receive an additional 1% compensation. Both front-end and back-end fees are legally required to be disclosed in a good faith estimate.

Points represent an amount as additional paid up-front fees to help buy down the interest rate of a loan. One point is equivalent to 1% of the loan amount. For every point paid, the interest rate may decrease by $1/_8$ to $1/_4$ of a percent. This range is a generalized estimate; the spread of rates varies widely from lender to lender. Rate spreads are dynamic, which means they may fluctuate with minor changes in the market. A rate quote may be good for a day or it may be good for only the moment. Lenders are able to provide exact quotes as specified on rate sheets. Points are beneficial for properties that are going to be held long-term because the reduction in interest rates has the potential to provide huge cost savings over the term of a loan. However, points do not offer much benefit for investors who plan to hold a property short-term. These investors would do better to pay the higher interest rate with no points since the breakeven point, which is the point at which it becomes beneficial to pay additional points, may be beyond the time for which the property is held. The breakeven point for paying points is calculated as follows:

$$\text{Breakeven} = \text{cost of points} \div \text{monthly savings}$$

Another consideration in deciding whether to pay points on a loan is the future value of the amount applied to points if it were invested in another property. An investor must consider whether buying down the interest over the life of a loan is more beneficial than using that money to invest in another property or asset over the life of the loan. Using the equation for present value, $PV = FV \div (1 + I)^N$ we solve for i as follows:

$$i = (FV \,/\, PV)^{(1/N)} - 1$$

Example:

An investor is trying to determine whether a $10,500 investment amount should be applied toward discount points for a mortgage loan or used to invest in another property. It has been determined that an average savings of $500 per month could be achieved over the 30-year life of the investment by buying down the interest rate. The total savings would be $180,000.

PV = the initial investment or cash flow out
FV = the amount of return expected or cash flow in
n = the number of years

$$i = (FV \:/\: PV)^{(1/N)} - 1$$
$$i = (\$180{,}000 \:/\: \$10{,}500)^{(1/30)} - 1$$
$$i = (17.14285714)^{(0.0333)} - 1$$
$$i = 1.099246194 - 1$$
$$i = .099246194$$
$$i = 9.92\%$$

From this calculation, we determine that an investor would have to earn a return of 9.92% or greater to receive the same or better benefit as using $10,500 to pay down the interest rate of the loan. If the investor could not earn a 9.92% return on a new investment, it would be more cost effective for the investor to apply the $10,500 to buying down the interest on the existing mortgage.

Prepayment Penalties

Prepayment penalties are the amount that some banks and lending institutions charge borrowers for repaying a loan prematurely. This type of penalty is usually assessed for larger commercial loans and multi-family loans. These institutions impose such penalties to prevent borrowers from refinancing with another institution, which means the original lender would lose the interest income associated with the loan. If, for example, an investor acquired a loan to purchase a multi-family unit at 8% interest and market rates decreased to 5%, that investor is likely to refinance the loan amount with another lender. With the repayment penalty, the investor has to consider the cost of refinancing with the new lender, as well as the cost of prepayment penalties imposed by the original lender. Prepayment penalties are most effective for the lender when they are assessed against loans in the early life of those loans since interest payments are often greatest during the early life of a loan. Prepayment penalties are determined in a variety of ways. Fee structures range from a simple declining penalty to more complex structures for commercial loans. Prepayment penalties are also assessed against loans to prevent a change of ownership. In the past, most loans were assumable, which means a loan could be assumed by or transferred to a third party without having to acquire a new loan. Under this system, a less responsible borrower could assume a loan that was acquired by a responsible borrower who makes timely payments. Though this type of assumption is no longer as commonplace, assumable loans still exist. However, most mortgages for single-family properties include a "due on sale" clause that specifies that the loan must be repaid in full before the sale or assumption of ownership. Prepayment penalties have the effect of creating an effective interest rate for the financing of the loan.

Example:

An investor purchases a multi-family property for $600,000 with the intention of renting the units for profit. The investor borrows $450,000 at 5.25% to make the purchase. After the purchase, the investor learns that the site of the property is included in plans for redevelopment. A development company is interested in developing the land on which the property sits. In the third year of ownership the development company makes the investor an offer for the property. The investor has an outstanding mortgage with prepayment penalties assessed as follows:

Prepay Loan in:	Prepayment Penalty
Year 1	6%
Year 2	5%
Year 3	4%
Year 4	2%
Year 5	0%

Before the investor can determine what would be considered a reasonable offer, the investor needs to determine how the prepayment penalty would affect the transaction. For the purposes of the example, we assume an interest only loan with no payments on the principal balance and no loan origination fees.

139

Purchase price = $600,000
Loan amount = $450,000
Interest rate = 5.25%
Turnaround time = 3 years

The interest paid is:

$$I = Prt$$
$$= \$450,000 * 5.25\% * 3$$
$$= \$450,000 * .0525 * 3$$
$$= \$70,875$$

The 3-year prepayment penalty as applied to the total loan amount is:

$$\text{Penalty} = 450,000 * 4\%$$
$$= 450,000 * .04$$
$$= 18,000$$

The total interest and penalty fee is: $70,875 + $18,000 = $88,875.

Though the investor choose to secure a loan at 5.25%, the prepayment penalty percentage creates an effective rate of 6.58% as follows:

$$r = I \div Pt$$
$$= \$88,875 \div (\$450,000 * 3)$$
$$= \$88,875 \div \$1,350,000$$
$$= 0.06583333$$
$$= 6.58\%$$

LEVERAGE

Leverage is the use of other people's money, which is also referred to as the OPM principle. Leverage in real estate presumes that the cost of other people's money is less than the return on the invested asset. When an investor borrows money from a bank or other financial institution for an investment, the investor is said to be using other people's money. By borrowing money, the investor creates a debt and the principle of leverage presumes that the cost of that debt is less than the return from the asset that the debt was used to acquire. If the cost of the debt is not less than the return, it is not advantageous for an investor to assume the loan because the investor will lose money.

Example:

The expected return on investment from a rental property is 10% of the investment amount. The investor borrows money to make the investment at a rate of 6.5%. The leverage is considered positive if the difference between the cost of funds and the return on assets (ROA) is positive. This difference is called the spread.

$$\text{Spread} = \text{ROA} - \text{cost of funds}$$
$$= 10\% - 6.5\%$$
$$= 3.5\%$$

If, on the other hand, the expected return from the asset was 5% and money was borrowed at 6.5% to purchase the asset, the leverage would be considered negative.

$$\text{Spread}$$
$$= 5\% - 6.5\%$$
$$= -1.5$$

Some investors make the mistake of highly leveraging an investment, assuming that it must make for a good investment since the investor is not required to put any money down. However, when the spread is negative and cash flow is negative, due to high leverage, a property cannot generate a positive return. The investor will be required to take funds from a cash reserve to make up the difference each month. If the investor has no cash reserve, the investment will be a total loss.

Debt Leverage

Other people's money can be acquired as either a debt or equity. Debt is most often acquired through borrowing money. Using debt as a source of financing usually requires the repayment of a loan with predetermined terms and conditions, such as interest rates, terms of repayment, prepayment penalties, application fees, and the like. The advantages of using debt for financing are that capital may be acquired at a lower cost than other forms of financing, such as equity, and debt is often more readily available for use than equity. Another advantage is that the interest applied to debt is tax deductible. Interest is treated as an expense of an investment for tax purposes. The interest charged for a debt has the effect of creating an effective interest rate that is lower than what would otherwise be assessed on a loan. This makes debt more cost effective than equity because the investor is further able to reduce the cost of borrowing. The disadvantage of using debt is that it must be serviced. When periodic payments are made on a loan, the loan is considered serviced.

Example:

A debt of $150,000 is acquired at 6.2% by an investor whose income falls in the 35% tax bracket. We want to determine the effective rate of interest, considering the tax deduction for interest on the loan.

$$\text{Loan amount} = \$150,000$$
$$\text{Interest rate} = 6.2\%$$
$$\text{Tax rate} = 35\%$$

The annual interest paid on the loan is:

$$I = Prt$$
$$= \$150,000 * .062 * 1$$
$$= \$9,300$$

The tax deduction is:

$$\$9,300 * .35$$

$$= \$3,255$$

The interest payment minus the tax deduction is:

$$\$9,300 - \$3,255 = \$6,045$$

The effective interest rate is:

$$r = I \div Pt$$
$$= \$6,045 \div (\$150,0000 * 1)$$
$$= 0.0403$$
$$= 4.03\%$$

The investor realizes a savings of $3,255 as a result of the tax deduction, and the effective tax rate is 4.03%.

When debt is used for financing, it reduces cash flow by the amount that is required to make monthly loan payments. When debt is used to finance income property, the financing should be structured such that the debt, after all expenses have been paid, is not cause for a negative cash flow. After all expenses have been paid a minimum 1:1 to 1:2 ratio of free cash should be left over.

Equity

Equity provides another source of funding for investments. Equity is money that is invested. Equity differs from debt since debt is money that is borrowed. Equity financing may be provided by any number of sources, but it often requires some type of partnership or the formation of a corporation. Private investors, business associates, friends, and family may provide an investor with equity financing. Some institutional investors are willing to provide funding for investments in the form of equity rather then loans. However, the institutional investor becomes a shareholder of the investment partnership or corporation. Funds provided by equity investors provide small investors with the leverage to purchase larger investment properties than they would otherwise be able to afford.

Equity investors typically require a minimum return on their investment dollars than are required with traditional financing. As shareholders, equity investors expect a share of any profits resulting from a sale of the investment property. Most large institutional investors finance only large projects for millions of dollars. Some of the largest institutional investors only engage projects over $5 million. Institutional investors often provide 80 to 90% of the required funding, so the small investor must be prepared to contribute a minimum of 10 to 20% of the funding.

The repayment of equity financing may be structured in any manner agreeable to the parties involved in the financing. An agreement may specify that payments be made quarterly, semi-annually, annually, or an agreement may specify that payment be made after a sale of the property. Profits may be shared based on the income of the property, capital gains, or a combination of both. This flexibility offered by equity financing minimizes the cash flow out of a property, which preserves cash for the investor, particularly in the early years of an investment when cash reserves may be low.

Institutional investors prefer to form partnerships with local investors who are familiar with the market in their particular location. Local investors have the advantage of knowing which areas are best suited for various projects. They are in a better position of assessing which areas are experiencing positive and strong growth and which areas are deteriorating and present a risk. Local investors are also in a better position to help with or carry out the functions of property management. Institutional investors have large pools of cash for investment purposes and are very selective in the properties they choose to finance. Since local investors have the advantages stated above, they are expected to be selective in choosing properties that have potential as a sound investment. Local investors must be prepared to provide a well-defined business plan with data specific to the property and the area, such as unemployment, rental rates, and vacancy rates, as compared to other properties. They should also be capable of selling themselves as professionals, with the potential to carry out the functions specified in the business plan.

PARTNERSHIPS

In addition to the type of partnership formed between small investors and large institutional investors as discussed above, partnerships may be formed between friends, business acquaintances, or family members. Financing may be achieved when these individuals combine their resources. Such partnerships may be structured in a number of ways. They may form either debt or equity partnerships, and partners may choose to play an active or passive role. The terms of repayment may be defined in a number of different ways as long as all partners are in agreement with the chosen method. One of the most challenging aspects of this type of partnership is finding a partner that one can work with. Partners need to have the right balance of temperament and respect to successfully work together.

If this type of individual partnership is funded by debt, a contractual agreement will specify that partners be repaid a fixed amount. The type and amount of payment may be specified as interest only, principal and interest, or it may specify that all payments be deferred until the property is sold. Regardless of the payment structure, the amount to be repaid is not based on the profitability of the business, but should be specified in a promissory note that is witnessed and recorded. Though such partnerships are engaged without recording such an instrument, it is in the best interest of the partner or partners who are loaning the funds to record the instrument, and they should be provided the option to do so. The debt may be financed by a loan that is secured by the property, some other form of collateral, or it may not be secured.

If debt financing is not used to fund the investment, equity financing may be established between partners. An equity partner shares the risk of the partnership, and if the partnership fails, the equity partner will likely lose on the investment. Likewise, if the investment profits, the equity partner also profits.

Partners may take either an active or passive role in the management and operation of the property. Partners with skills beneficial to the partnership offer the benefit of providing those skills without additional cost to the partnership. However, partners that lack skills may cost the partnership, and they should be allowed to take a passive role, where their only contribution is investment funding.

Partners must be able to work together to achieve the goals of the partnership. A partnership requires collaboration and cooperation, but disputes may arise. The objective of the partners is not so much to avoid disputes, but to be capable of resolving such differences peacefully. One way to avoid unnecessary disputes and conflicts is to clarify the duties and responsibilities of each partner and to allow each partner to work toward his or her goals within a predetermined time. People are often quick to criticize and micromanage other people's work and performance, but that may spell disaster for the individual relationships, as well as the partnership. Even when it seems that partners have found that balance of temperament and respect to work well together, the relationship can fall apart for any number of reasons. Partners need to consider how a potential failure of an investment will affect the relationship between the individual partners before forming a partnership, particularly when the partnership is formed with family members.

Equated Time

Many times, when two or more individuals decide to invest in a businesses opportunity, they avoid the formal procedure of forming a corporation and instead operate as a partnership. A partnership agreement specifies, among other things, an agreed upon division of profits. A method of determining the division of profits involves a fixed or determinable ratio. Since a partnership may include two or more partners, the method of distribution is more complicated than an ordinary proportion or ratio, such as $^1/_3$ for each of three partners or ½ for each of two partners. The division of profits may be based on the amount of investment made by each of the partners. This requires the calculation of a continued proportion, such as 2:3:5 for each of three partners. If the amount of investment remains constant throughout the year, the division of profits involves a simple division in proportion to the numbers in the series 2:3:5. However, if the amount of each partner's investment fluctuates throughout the year, the average investment by each partner must be determined using equated time.

Equated time considers the length of time that an investment has been kept in a business. It may be assumed that a dollar of investment left in a business for two months is twice as effective as a dollar of investment for one month. The length of time that an investment amount is left in a business, unchanged, must be determined. Many partnerships provide for investments to occur only at the beginning or end of a monthly period. During this period, amounts may be deducted or added to the investment, so that months are used as the basis for comparison for investment amounts. While a monthly basis is common, days may also be used. In either case, the net amount of each partner's original investment must be multiplied by the number of months (or days) that this amount remains unchanged during the year. If the amount of any of partner's investment changes during the month, the net amount of each partner's investment must be recalculated. The new amount is then multiplied by the number of months (or days) for which it remains unchanged.

Example 1:

Two individual investors form a partnership, and the investment profits are $5,236.50 for the year. Partners A and B realize changes in investment as follows:

	Investor A		Investor B	
Jan 1	Balance	5,000		8,000
March 1	Added	2,000	Withdrew	-1,000
June 1	Withdrew	-1,000	-	
July 1	-		Added	2,000
Sept 1	Added	1,000	Added	1,000
Dec 1	Withdrew	-1,500	Withdrew	-1,000
Total Investment:		-500		2,000

Profits from the partnership are to be divided according to the amount invested by each partner. Each partner's investment fluctuates during the year. The average investment by each partner during the year is calculated using equated time. The original investment of each partner is multiplied by the number of months for which the investment remained unchanged during the year. When an amount is changed, each partner's investment, after the change, is multiplied by the number of months for which the investments remain unchanged. This product is called month-dollars of capital. When days are used instead of months, the product is called day-dollars. The month-dollar investment for each partner is calculated as follows:

Investor A			
	Investment	Months in Business	Month-Dollar
Jan 1	5,000	2	10,000
Mar 1	7,000	3	21,000
June 1	6,000	3	18,000
July 1			0
Sept 1	7,000	3	21,000
Dec 1	5,500	1	5,500
Sum of Month-Dollar			75,500

Investor B			
	Investment	Months in Business	Month-Dollar
Jan 1	8,000	2	16,000
Mar 1	7,000	4	28,000
June 1			0
July 1	9,000	2	18,000
Sept 1	10,000	3	30,000
Dec 1	9,000	1	9,000
Sum of Month-Dollar			101,000

The equated time ratio of each partner's investment to the total investment is calculated as the ratio of sum months-dollars for each partner to the sum of month-dollars for all partners.

The sum of Investor A and Investor B month-dollar investments
$$= \$75,500 + \$101,000$$
$$= \$176,500$$

Investor A's share of profits
$$= \text{Investor A's month-dollar} \div \text{total month-dollars} * \text{profit}$$
$$= 75,500 \div 176,500 * 5,236.50$$
$$= 2,239.98$$

Investor B's share of the profit
$$= 101,000 \div 176,500 * 5,236.50$$
$$= 2,996.52$$

Blended Financing

In the purchase of income properties, particularly large purchases, investors may partner with several sources of funding, both debt and equity partners. An investor may, for example, secure funding from a mortgage lender, an equity investor, a bank, and the investor's own cash reserves. Each of the funding sources is most likely to charge differing rates for the use of their money. To determine the overall rate, a blended rate must be calculated. A blended rate is also known as a weighted average cost of capital (WACC). The WACC is the average rate of return required by all creditors and investors. The use of WACC for determining thresholds may be used for both large- and small-scale investments

A business's WACC enables the business to determine its threshold for future investments. As an example, a real estate company with a portfolio of properties computes its WACC at 6.5%. The company seeks to purchase another property with a similar cost structure for investment funding. The company decides not to invest in another property unless they are convinced that the property could earn a minimum of 6.5%. If the expected return does not meet the 6.5% threshold, the company saves its resources for a more favorable investment opportunity since anything less means the cost of financing will exceed the income received from it and the company would lose money.

The WACC is calculated as follows:

WACC = proportion of debt * cost of debt + proportion of equity * cost of equity

$$WACC = \frac{B}{B+S} R_B + \frac{S}{B+S} R_S$$

where:
B = the value of bonds or debt
S = the value of stocks or equity
R_B = the cost of debt or interest rate of debt
R_S = the cost of equity or the expected return on equity

Example:

An investment firm has a real estate portfolio in the millions of dollars. The total outstanding debts of the firm are $37 million, and the total outstanding equity is $8 million. The average cost of the debt is 7%, and the average cost of equity is 10%. The WACC of the firm is calculated as follows:

$$B = \text{value of debts} = \$37M$$
$$S = \text{value of equity} = \$8$$
$$R_B = \text{the cost of debt} = 7\%$$
$$R_S = \text{the cost of equity} = 10\%$$

$$\text{WACC} = (B \div B + S) * R_B + (S \div B + S) * R_S$$
$$= (\$37M \div \$37M + \$8M) * .07 + (\$8M \div \$37M + \$8M) * .10$$
$$= 0.822 * .07 + 0.178 * .10$$
$$= .0576 + .00178$$
$$= .059$$
$$= 5.9\%$$

Options

Options are an agreement between investors and another party to gain control of assets without having to take legal title to the assets. Options provide investors with the legal right to purchase control of an asset at some predetermined price. Options are used in the stock market to gain control of the right to either purchase or sell securities. Stock options are valued by standards established by the Black-Scholes model, which has time as a primary variable. Investors must exercise their rights of a stock option within a specified period of time. If the right is exercised at the right time, the investor stands to gain; however, it is also possible for an option to expire with no worth, and the investor will lose on investment amount. Options in real estate work the same way. An investor is provided the legal right to purchase a parcel of property at a predetermined price within a specified time. In real estate, the seller of options may require that investors take on additional obligations of the property, such as paying the interest and taxes on a property. These additional obligations are negotiable. If an option is not exercised within the specified time frame, the option will expire worthless. Under options, an investor's legal interest in a property is typically transferable. This is what gives the investor the right to gain control of the property without having to take title to it. The investor may transfer title to a third party before having to take title to it. Options provide a tool for investors to purchase property with very little cash and limit their risk to only the premium used to purchase the option. Premiums may be as low as 1% of the purchase price. If the investor fails to exercise the right to purchase property under an option, the option expires worthless, and the only loss to the investor is the premium paid for the option. The value of an option is relative to the value of the property being sought. Some real estate is valuable enough to command a premium of tens of thousands of dollars. There are no standards for establishing a premium amount for real estate options. The price is negotiated between the parties that have an interest in the property.

Options may be used by real estate developers to acquire the right to properties to be built on without having to take title to the properties until the construction begins. The developer is provided with a recordable interest in the property. A carefully drafted option agreement provides the developer with the right to build on the property at a specified and predetermined price. Once the developer engages in a purchase agreement to build on the lot, the option is exercised and legal title is granted. Interest and taxes begin to accrue with the signing of the purchase agreement. However, the option allows for these costs to be deferred until construction begins on the lot. This minimizes the developer's cash flow allowing them to retain the otherwise out flow of cash for other investment opportunities. As such a developer is able to gain control of property for only a portion of what would be required if the developer financed the purchase of the property through traditional bank financing, which would require about 20% down payment. This type of leverage is the real benefit of using options. Another advantage of using options is that the developer is not burdened with the cost of owning the property if the property cannot be sold. The developer only loses the money used to purchase the option. If the lot were purchased instead of engaging in an option agreement, the sale of the lot would trigger a tax increase on the property due to the higher assessed value. The value of a finished lot is much higher than the lot when the developer starts to improve it.

DEPRECIATION FOR REAL ESTATE INVESTMENTS

Investment real estate is any property purchased or leased for the purpose of producing income. The property may be a rental property or a business entity. Depreciation for real estate investments is the depreciation allowance provided by the IRS. This type of depreciation is not to be confused with the depreciation used in appraisals. Both types of depreciation provide a method of accounting for the loss in value of property, but they serve two separate and distinct purposes and involve differing calculations. The IRS depreciation allowance is a paper deduction, designed to encourage investment. This depreciation allows taxpayers to recover the cost of depreciable property by deducting the depreciable portion of the property from their income taxes, thereby reducing the tax burden on the income they receive.

The deduction of depreciation for real estate investments has no relationship to the physical condition of the property for which the deduction is allowed. This is in contrast to the depreciation used in appraisals. The deduction taken in the cost approach method of appraisals is a measure of the difference between a new structure and the existing condition of a structure being valued in the appraisal.

The IRS depreciation expense for real estate investments is a way of deducting the costs of improvements to a parcel of land over a period of time. This type of depreciation is only allowed for business properties and income producing properties. Though land itself is not depreciable, structures and improvements on the land are depreciable. The depreciation allowance is calculated using the straight-line method of depreciation, which allows taxpayers to deduct an equal amount of depreciation expense each year from their income. The IRS has established a 27(1/2) year depreciation period for residential rental properties and a 39-year depreciation period for nonresidential income producing properties. The depreciable basis for such a deduction is often the total purchase price of the property minus the land value.

The annual depreciation allowance is calculated as:

IRS annual depreciation allowance = depreciable basis ÷ number of allowable years

In most instances:
Depreciable basis = total purchase price of a property – value of the land

LEASING REAL ESTATE INVESTMENT PROPERTY

There are several types of leases that may be drawn for investment properties. The two most typical lease arrangements include a percentage lease and a variable lease. A percentage lease is typically used for retail property to proportion the income from the property between the leaser and leaseholder. This type of lease provides for a proportional sharing of monthly or annual gross sales made on the leased premises. The lease agreement will typically indicate a base monthly rent plus a percentage of gross sales in excess of a certain amount to be proportioned.

A variable lease provides for rent to vary at specified times during the term of the lease. A variable lease is also referred to as an index lease. A variable lease agreement allows for the adjustment of rent according to changes in a price index, such as the consumer price index.

CHAPTER 4

REAL ESTATE MATHEMATICS

LAND MEASURES

Understanding real estate requires an understanding of measures used in defining a parcel of land. The area of a parcel of land may be described in a number of ways, almost all of which require some understanding of geometric principles. It is not the responsibility of investors or property owners to measure and document land measurements. There are professionals trained to provide land descriptions and to provide accurate land measures. However, investors and real estate professionals need to understand how such measurements are determined and expressed. They also need to know how to convert among various methods of describing a parcel of land.

In the U.S., a parcel of land is expressed in terms of acres and square feet. A square foot is the most commonly used unit of measurement since it is used for comparisons, and it is also used in zoning laws to prescribe building footprints and building areas. In other nations, the metric unit hectare may be used. One hectare is just short of 2.5 acres.

Plats and Maps

Any person involved in real estate should be able to comprehend and interpret information specified on plats and maps that uniquely describe a parcel of property. This knowledge is necessary to locate and identify properties. Plats and maps may be referenced for a description of both large and small lots, as well as residential and commercial parcels of land.

Boundary Lines

Each parcel of land is completely enclosed by its boundary lines. Boundary lines may or may not be visible on the ground, but are clearly identified on plats of land. Any physical evidence of boundary lines is known as a monument. The boundary lines that enclose a parcel of land have both length and direction, which are indicated on a plat alongside each boundary line. The length of boundary lines is usually expressed in feet, measured to the nearest hundredth foot. Corners mark the ends of boundary lines, and the directions of boundary lines are measured by the line's bearings.

A bearing is a situation or the direction of a point or object with respect to another situation, or direction. Bearings are identified on plats as either north or south compass directions along with acute angle measurements. The angle measurement measures the angle between compass north and the bearing line or compass south and the bearing line.

Figure 1 shows a circle with boundary lines that correspond to the compass directions, north, south, east, and west. The opening shown in the figure represents an angle of 45 degrees, 0 minutes, and 0 seconds, represented as 45° 0′ 0″. In the geometry of circles, measurements are as follows:

1 degree =	1/360th of a circle
1 minute =	1/60th of a degree
1 second =	1/60th of a minute

As such, 45° are the equivalent of $^{45}/_{360}$ or $^{1}/_{8}$ of a circle.

Boundary lines form angles that divide the circle into quadrants: northeast (NE), northwest (NW), southeast (SE), and southwest (SW). The north-south line represents a meridian.

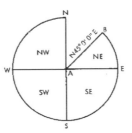

Figure 1: Boundary Lines

Like with the circle, the bearing of any boundary line on a plat may be identified by its stated angle, measured from compass north, south, east, or west of a north-south meridian, depending on the compass quadrant in which it falls. The quadrant of a boundary line is specified as a prefix and suffix to the stated angle. The angle specified in the circle at Figure 1 along line AB is N45 0'0"E, which indicates that the line falls in the northeast quadrant at 45°.

Bearings may be measured either clockwise or counter clockwise, but not in both directions on the same plat. Changing directions from clockwise to counter clockwise on a plat has the effect of changing the prefix and suffix of boundary lines, but the value of angles remains unchanged. Figure 2 shows two representations of the same lot. However, the prefix and suffix of the angular bearings are opposite, even though the bearings, themselves, are the same. The leftmost representation of the lot provides measurements from a clockwise direction while the rightmost representation of the lot provides measurements from a counter clockwise direction.

**Figure 2: Clockwise & Counter Clockwise
Angular Buildings**

Arc Lines

Boundary lines are not always represented with straight lines. Boundary lines may also be indicated as arcs. An arc is a portion of a curved line formed from a circle. The radius of the circle is a measure of the distance from the center of the circle to a point on the perimeter of the circle. The radius is the same no matter where it is measured on a circle. The angle formed by any two lines that intersect at the center of a circle and extend to the perimeter of the circle is represented by delta (Δ). An arc, its radius, and delta are shown on plats when an arc forms a boundary line. The arc formed by points N, A, and B in Figure 1 has a radius of length AB and delta equal to 45°.

Boundary Descriptions

Figure 3 shows a parcel of land that is identified as Lot 1 on a plat. The description reads, "Beginning at the iron pipe on the north side of Fortune Boulevard, 200′ from its intersection with the easterly boundary of Fame Street, on a bearing S88°5′14″E for a distance of 98.06′ thence for a distance of 137.98′ on bearing S09°5′18″W to the north side of Fortune Boulevard; thence 108.16′ on bearing S88°5′14″E to the beginning."

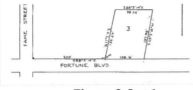

Figure 3: Lot 1

When a lot has an easement on it and the easement lies completely within the boundaries of the lot, the easement will usually be outlined with dotted lines. If the easement runs along the boundary line of the lot, a solid boundary line on one side and a dotted line on the other side outline the easement. Both representations of an easement are shown at Figure 4.

Figure 4: Easement Representation on a Plot

When a plat is too large to be completely represented on a page, a continuation of the portion of the plat that extends beyond the edge of the page may be displayed in available white space on the same page. Figure 5 shows a plat that cannot be fully displayed on a single page. The portion of the plat that extends beyond lot 12 is drawn on the left side of the page. As such, lot 12 appears twice on the page as reference. The utility easement on Lot 12 is also shown in both renditions of the lot. Clearly, only one lot on the plat has an easement on it.

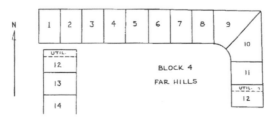

Figure 5: Continuation of a Plat

Front Feet

Land may be described in terms of its front feet. Front feet are a measure of road frontage. As the term implies, front feet describe the dimensions at the front of a parcel of property. It does not consider the depth of a property. In areas zoned for commercial use, front feet may be used to express the amount of exposure to passing traffic. The more exposure or front feet that a parcel of property provides, the more valuable the property may be. When two properties are similar in location and construction and measure the same total area, the property that is described as having the greatest number of front feet is thought to have the greatest exposure and will command a higher price. Municipalities, when determining a property owner's share of the cost to install or maintain a sewer line or other such installations on a property, may also use this type of measurement.

Legal Land Descriptions

The land description of a property is any information that a skilled, professional surveyor uses in defining a parcel of property and marking each corner of the property. There are four accepted methods of legally describing a parcel of property: monuments and markings, recorded plat of subdivision, metes and bounds, and the rectangular survey system.

Monuments and Markings

The monuments and markings method of legally describing a property is also called, simply, monuments. This is the crudest of all methods since it relies on such things as streams, trees, boulders, or other natural monuments to determine the outline of boundaries for a property. This method of surveying is not likely to be practiced today unless, in the rare instance, a survey is required for a parcel of property that has never been surveyed before.

Recorded Plat of Subdivision (Lot, Block)

The recorded plat of subdivision method of legally describing a parcel of property is also referred to as lot, block, tract, or simply lot, block. This method of describing a property requires that a surveyor record a particular parcel of property in the subdivision in which the property is located. The recorded plat contains the lot and block identification number, as well as the name of the subdivision and county in which the subdivision is located.

Metes and Bounds Description

The metes and bounds method of legally describing a property provides measurements (metes) and direction (bounds) of a property An understanding of the geometry of a circle must be understood to interpret the directional aspects of this type of description. Each description has a point of beginning (POB) and turning points, which should be interpreted as the exact centers of circles.

The geometry of a circle dictates that a circle has 360°. Starting at any point on a circle and following the perimeter of the circle until the same point is reached is a rotation of 360°. If a circle is divided into four equal parts with a line from north to south and a line from west to east, both lines intersecting at the center of the circle, the circle is divided into quadrants. Each quadrant of the circle measures 90°.

In metes and bounds descriptions, the direction from the center of a circle can only be north, south, east, or west. The first (or primary) direction indicator from the POB is always specified as either a northern or southern direction with a rotation, expressed in degrees, in an eastern or western direction. The direction of the rotation is the secondary direction indicator. It is followed by distance measurement. As an example, North 32° 60' 15" East 145 feet specifies a straight line north of the POB with a rotation in the eastern direction. The rotation is specified as 32 degrees, 60 feet, and 15 inches at which point a second POB is created. A straight line is then drawn connecting the first POB to the second POB for the length specified by the distance measurement.

A metes and bounds description must have a definite and stable starting point, and from this point, the description must recite the course and distance of each boundary line. The boundary lines must run continuously from one point or corner to another until the starting point is reached, such that a closed area is defined. A description that does not return to the starting point to form a closed area is seriously defective. Metes and bound descriptions often provide statements regarding the acreage or square footage of the parcel of property, such as the description given in the section, "Boundary Descriptions." However, when no survey has been made of a property, the description may contain general bearings and distances. As an example, "Beginning at an iron pipe on the north side of Easy Street, northwest to an oak tree, thence northeast to a pile of rocks, thence southeast to a fence corner thence southwest to the point of origin and containing ____ acres more or less" is a description for a parcel of land for which no survey has been performed. This type of description always ends with the phrase 'more or less' to indicate that the exact acreage cannot be determined without a survey.

Rectangular Survey System

Another land description is known as the rectangular survey system. This system is also called the government survey method, and it is used primarily in the Midwestern and western states of the U.S. This system is based on lines of longitude and latitude, which form a checkerboard pattern. North-south lines are called meridians, and there are 36 meridians in the U.S. The curvature of the earth causes principal meridians to converge as they extend north or south of the equator, so correction lines are run every 24 miles. Lines of latitude are called base lines. On each side of principal meridian lines, numbered squares are formed to create townships as follows:

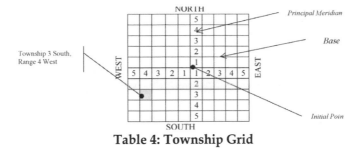

Table 4: Township Grid

A township is a square with six miles on each side, which equates to 36 square miles. As such, a township may be easily divided into 36 sections. A section is a square with 1 mile on each side, which equates to 1 square mile. A line of townships running north to south is called a range. A township is identified by counting townships north or south of a named base line and east or west of a principal meridian. The sequence of numbering sections of a township is as follows:

Township 3 South, Range 4 West

6	5	4	3	2	1
7	8	9	10	11	12
18	17	16	15	14	13
19	20	21	22	23	24
30	29	28	27	26	25
31	32	33	34	35	36

Each section is identifiable by its number, township, and range. Each of the 36 sections shown is 640 acres and may be further divided into quarters, halves, and other, smaller tracts. Constructing vertical and horizontal lines within existing tracts forms new tracts. Each quarter section measures one-half mile on each side and contains 160 acres. Each half-section measures one-quarter mile and contains 40 acres. Quarter sections are identified by the compass quadrants NE, SE, SW, and NW. Eight monuments mark sections, one at each corner and one midway between each corner monument.

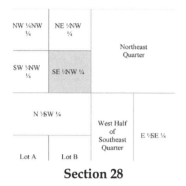

Section 28

Under this system, each parcel of land can be easily identified, and no two parcels of land will ever have the same identification. The legal description of properties under the rectangular survey should be interpreted by beginning at the end of the description and working back from right to left. The shaded parcel of land should be identified as:

The Southeast ¼ of the Northwest ¼; Section 28; Township 3, South; Range 4, West
SE ¼ of the NW ¼, S.28, T.3S, R.4W

In working with land measurements, one needs to know how to perform conversions between measurements. Some useful conversions that may be used are as follows:

Acres to Square Feet	multiply by	43,560
Square Feet to Acres	multiply by	.000023
Acres to Square Miles	multiply by	.0015625
Square Miles to Acres	multiply by	640
Acres to Hectares	multiply by	.4046856
Hectares to Acres	multiply by	2.471054
Acres to Square Meters	multiply by	4046.86
Square Meters to Acres	multiply by	.000247
Square Meters to Square Feet	multiply by	10.76391
Square Feet to Square Meters	multiply by	.092903
Meters to Feet	multiply by	3.2808399
Feet to Meters	multiply by	.3048

Example 1:

A lot measuring 90 feet by 150 feet was sold for $57.50 per front foot. The selling price is calculated as follows:

Frontage is always specified as the first dimension in property measurements.

$$90 \text{ ft.} * \frac{\$57.50}{\text{ft.}} = \$5,175.00$$

Example 2:

A triangular shaped lot with 200 feet of frontage and 217.8 feet in depth is sold for $4,000 per acre. The selling price is calculated as follows:

$$\text{Area of a triangle} = \frac{1}{2} * B * A$$
$$= \frac{1}{2} * 200 \text{ ft.} * 217.8 \text{ ft.}$$
$$= 21,780 \text{ ft}^2$$
Average is calculated as follows:
$$21,780 \text{ ft.}^2 * .000023 = 0.50094 \text{ acres}$$
The selling price is
$$0.50094 \text{ acres} * (\$4,000/\text{acre})$$
$$=\$2,003.76$$

Example 3:

A farm has 75 acres of timber. In addition, 37.5% of the farm is pasture, $^3/_{16}$ of the farm is planted corn, and $^1/_{16}$ of the farm contains structures. The total acreage of the farm is calculated as follows:

From the table of aliquant parts, we know that $37.5\% = {}^3/_8$
Total acreage = $^3/_8$ total acreage + $^3/_{16}$ total acreage + $^1/_{16}$ total acreage + 75 acres
= $^6/_{16}$ total acreage + $^3/_{16}$ total acreage + $^1/_{16}$ total acreage + 75 acres

$$= 10/16 \text{ total acreage} + 75 \text{ acres}$$
$$\text{total acreage} - \frac{5}{8} \text{ total acreage} = 75 \text{ acres}$$
$$\frac{3}{8} \text{ total acreage} = 75 \text{ acres}$$
$$\text{total acreage} = 75 \text{ acres} * \frac{8}{3}$$
$$= 200 \text{ acres}$$

Example 4:

A commercial lot that is ¼ acre and 100 feet deep is purchased for $1 per square foot. The property is sold after realizing a 50% profit on the original investment amount. $3,400 is paid in taxes, $65 is paid as a survey fee, and a 10% brokerage fee is paid on the final sale. The front footage for which the property is sold is calculated as follows:

$$1 \text{ acre} = 43{,}560 \text{ sq. feet}$$
$$\text{¼ acre} = 10{,}890 \text{ sq. feet}$$
$$\text{cost} = \$10{,}890$$
$$\text{profit} = 50\% \text{ of the cost} = \$5{,}445$$
$$\text{selling price} = \$16{,}335 + \$3{,}400 + \$65 + (10\% \text{ of the selling price})$$
$$\text{selling price} = \$19{,}800 + (0.10 * \text{selling price})$$
$$(1 - 0.10) * \text{selling price} = \$19{,}800$$
$$\text{selling price} = \$19{,}800 \div .90$$
$$= \$22{,}000$$

The area of the property is:

$$A = L * W$$
$$10{,}890 \text{ square feet} = 100 \text{ ft} * w$$
$$w = 108.90 \text{ front feet}$$

$$\$22{,}000 \div 108.9$$
$$= \$202.0202$$

The property value is $202.02 per front foot.

REAL PROPERTY

Real property is any parcel of land, all improvements to the land, and the rights to all things under the surface and in the air above the land. Real property is classified in three general categories: public, quasi-public, and private. Public property is owned by government entities. Quasi-public property is privately owned property that is dedicated to the public, such as property owned by utility companies. Private property is held by individuals for profit or pleasure. Though a property may be privately owned, the owner's rights may be subject to limitations imposed by governments for the good of the public. Limitations may include those imposed through eminent domain, police power, taxation, and escheat.

- Eminent domain provides that the sovereign state may seize private property for public use. This right may be granted at any level of government and may be extended to private companies when it is determined to be for the public good.

- Police power is the right of states to make reasonable rules for the use and enjoyment of property when it is for the good of the public. Police power includes zoning ordinances and other such restrictions.

- Taxation is the right of states to tax property and to deprive the owner of ownership for the nonpayment of taxes.

- Escheat is the process of reverting property to the state when persons legally entitled to the property fail to make claim to the property or when no heirs to a property can be found.

Freehold Estates

When an individual owns a parcel of property, the individual is said to hold the property in fee. This differentiates ownership from right of possession, such as that provided under a lease agreement. When an individual's interest in a parcel of land lasts for at least a lifetime, that interest is considered a freehold estate. Freehold estates may be further classified as estates of inheritance and life estates. An estate of inheritance continues beyond the life of the owner and descends to the owner's heirs upon death. A life estate extends only for the lifetime of the owner. When an owner holds freehold interest, the owner is said to hold property in seisin. Seisin is the procession of real estate with the intention of claiming at least a lifetime interest.

Fee Simple Estates

The largest and best type of estate in real property is fee simple. Fee simple estates may be subjected to eminent domain, police power, taxation, and escheat, as well as claims of creditors or surviving spouse's rights. Even so, fee simple represents the least limited interest that an individual may hold in private property. The owner may do virtually anything that he or she wants with the property so long as the rights of others are not violated. The owner may sell the property, build upon it, let it sit idle, or do any number of things subject to the limitations indicated above. Fee simple estates may be absolute or conditional. Fee simple absolute is the most common form of interest in real property. Interest in the property is without limitation by the grant, which created it. Fee simple conditional interest is granted under the condition that some future event happens as specified by the grant. As an example, a father conveys property to his son under the condition that the son completes college by his twenty-fifth birthday; otherwise, the title reverts to the father or all the father's heirs.

When an individual is the single owner to a fee simple title, the owner is said to hold the property in severalty. When two or more individuals share the title, they are said to be concurrent owners. There are three basic concurrent estates: tenancy by entireties, joint tenancy, and tenancy in common.

Tenancy by Entireties

Tenancy by the entireties is a form of estate, which exists only with married couples in a limited number of states. This type of tenancy is based on the common law concept that dictates that a husband and wife are one person. It does not exist in community property states. A deed must be made to both the husband and the wife while the couple is married for this type of estate to exist. It cannot be established prior to a marriage. In the event of death of one of the spouses, the surviving spouse receives fee in simple title to the property. Neither spouse may sell or otherwise dispose of the property without the signature of the other spouse. Neither party can force a partition of the property. Creditors are prohibited from attaching to such property unless the creditor is creditor to both spouses. Should the couple divorce, the tenancy by the entities is dissolved, and the spouses become tenants in common. Some states require that such tenancy be specifically stated in the face of the granting instrument at the time of the grant. In other states, it exists automatically unless the spouses specifically take title in some other form.

Joint Tenancy

Joint tenancy is interest held by two or more individuals simultaneously. It has four utilities: time, interest, title, and possession. The tenants must hold identical interest, simultaneously acquired at the same time, in the same instrument, with all interests commencing at the same time. One estate exists with each person considered to be the owner of the whole estate. Upon the death of one of the joint tenants, the deceased tenant's interest in the property passes to his or her heirs, unless the instrument granting joint tenancy specifically indicates otherwise.

Tenancy in Common

Tenancy in common is interest held by two or more individuals, but the interest is granted by separate and distinct titles with a unity of possession. Owners may acquire their interests from different individuals or from the same individual. The owners need not have identical interests at the same time. Each tenant holds an undivided interest, is responsible for expenses of the property in proportion to his or her interest in the property, and should receive any profit in the property in proportion to his her interest. A tenant in common may dispose of all or part of their interest in the property without disturbing the tenancies of the other tenants. Upon the death of a tenant, the tenant's interest passes to the tenant's heirs, not the surviving tenants.

Valuation (Market Value)

Real property valuation falls in the field of appraisal since an appraiser is typically hired to estimate the market value of real property. Market value is defined as the most probable price that should bring in an open and competitive market under any condition requisite to a fair sale, assuming the buyer and seller are both acting prudently and knowledgeably and that the price is not affected by undue stimulus. The three approaches to estimating the value of real property include the sales comparison approach, the cost depreciation approach, and the income capitalization approach.

The Sales Comparison Approach to Valuation

The sales comparison approach is based on the assumption that a knowledgeable buyer will pay no more for a property than the cost of acquiring a similar substitute property. The value of property is estimated by reviewing recent sales of comparable properties. These comparables provide an indication of the price buyers are willing to pay in a competitive market. The sales of chosen comparables must meet standards. First, the sale of the property must have occurred recently in the same market area where the appraised property is located. Secondly, the comparable properties must be similar to the appraised property. However, no two properties are exactly alike, and adjustments must be made for any differences between the appraised property and the comparable properties.

Adjustments are made to the comparable properties, not the appraised property, to achieve the maximum similarity. The comparable property is adjusted to make it as similar as possible to the appraised property. If the comparable property is inferior in some aspect or feature to the appraised property, an upward adjustment is made to the comparable property. An upward adjustment adds the value of the difference and a downward adjustment deducts the value of the difference. If the comparable property is superior in some aspect or feature, a downward adjustment is made to the comparable property. An appraiser considers comparable feature of both properties, considers each feature for adjustment, one feature at a time, and then totals the adjustments.

The value of vacant lots is estimated by comparing it to similar neighboring lots. The cost per square footage and cost per front footage are the most common units of measurement for comparison. These measures of comparison provide a method of equalizing any variations in value due to size and shape. Often appraisers use weighted measures in which the comparable properties that are most similar to the appraised property are given more weight.

The Cost Depreciation Approach to Valuation

The cost depreciation approach, also called the cost approach, is based on the assumption that a knowledgeable buyer will pay no more for a property than the cost of acquiring a similar property and constructing an equivalent structure. The maximum value of the property is measured relative to the cost of acquiring an equivalent site to reproduce the structure as if it were new and subtracting any accrued depreciation.

Value of a property = Reproduction cost of a new structure – accrued depreciation + value of the site

The reproduction cost of a new structure is the amount that would be required to duplicate the building being appraised. Sometimes an appraiser will use the replacement cost of a new structure rather than the reproduction cost of a new structure. The replacement cost of a new structure takes into account the cost of improvements that would provide the same functional utility as the appraised structure but with the cost of modern building techniques and building materials that most closely resemble those of the original materials used in the older, appraised structure.

Accrued depreciation is the total depreciation that has accumulated over the years of a structure's existence. Depreciation is the loss in value of the appraised structure. Depreciation may be due to a number of circumstances, including physical deterioration, functional obsolesce, or external obsolesce. The appraiser estimates the dollar value of depreciation and subtracts that amount from the reproduction cost of a new structure. Accrued depreciation is the loss in value between the existing structure and an exact duplicate in new condition.

The site or land on which the structure sits is not depreciated in the cost depreciation approach. As such, land value is estimated as if the site were vacant. Only structures are depreciated.

Reproduction costs are typically estimated as per square foot of the structures. Certain publications are published for the purpose of providing estimates of the cost per square foot of living areas, garages, and other structures, based on the types of materials used and the quality of construction for the property being appraised. The outside dimensions of structures are used for estimates of measures of square footage, and the square footage of varying types of structures are measured and estimated separately. For example, heated and air conditioned living areas are appraised separately from garages.

Depreciation is estimated using the straight-line method of depreciation or the age-life method of depreciation. The straight-line method of depreciation spreads the total depreciation over the estimated economic life of a structure in equal, annual amounts. This method of depreciation allows for an equal amount of value to be depreciated each year until the economic life is exhausted. All structures have an economic life. Economic life is expressed in years and provides an estimate of the time that a property can be profitably useful. Straight-line depreciation is estimated by dividing the reproduction cost of a structure by the number of years of useful life.

Cost Approach Straight Line Depreciation

The cost approach method provides for the following estimates:

Annual depreciation:	Reproduction cost of a new structure ÷ Years of useful life
Accrued depreciation:	Annual depreciation * Actual age of the structure
The value of a property:	Reproduction cost of a new structures – Accrued depreciation + Value of the land

Cost Approach Age-Life Depreciation

In actual practice more appraisers use the age life method of depreciation, which takes the condition of a structure into account. The age life method provides a ratio of a property's effective age to its economic life. An effective age is an age estimate based on the condition of the property. As an example, two similar properties may be 10 years old and share the same useful life of 20 years. However, one property has been well maintained during its existing useful life and one has not. The well maintained property may be estimated to have an effective age equal to or close to its actual age, while the poorly maintained property may be estimated to have an effective age that is less than its actual age. The age-life method provides for the following estimates:

Annual depreciation:	Reproduction cost of a new structure ÷ Years of useful life
Accrued depreciation:	Effective age ÷ Total economic life
The value of a property:	Reproduction cost of a new structures − Accrued depreciation + Value of the land

Depreciation may be expressed as a percent. As such, total depreciation is 100%, and a structure that is 100% depreciated has no economic value.

The Income Capitalization Approach to Valuation

The income capitalization approach uses a capitalization rate and projections of net operating income in estimating property value. The income capitalization approach is the primary approach used in appraising income-producing properties and for comparing possible investments. This approach provides a method of measuring the cash flow of the projected income of income producing properties. An estimated market value is determined based on the present worth of the income property's future income. The cost approach method provides for the following estimates:

Net operating Income	Capitalization rate * Value
Accrued depreciation:	Annual depreciation * Actual age of the structure
Estimated value of a property:	Net operating income ÷ Capitalization rate

Net operating income is the income from an income producing property or business minus all operating expenses. Operating expenses fall into three general categories: fixed expenses, variable expenses, and reserves for replacement. Fixed operating expenses are expenses that remain constant. In the case of income producing properties, fixed operating expenses are expenses that remain constant irrespective of any vacancies. Such expenses include property taxes and hazard insurance. Variable operating expenses are expenses that vary with the operation of the business. Variable expenses may include such things as maintenance costs, supplies, and utilities. Reserves for replacement are reserve amounts that are used to provide the periodic replacement of structural components, such as roofing, heating, and air conditioning, which wear at a faster rate than other structural components.

REAL ESTATE DEPRECIATION

Most people anticipate that real estate will increase in value over time. This increase in value is known as appreciation. Investors sometimes study historic market data in an effort to predict rates of appreciation. Land is thought to appreciate since it is considered indestructible, immovable, and non-homogeneous. Buildings and other structures that are placed on the land are considered wasting assets and may decrease in value over time. This decrease in value is known as depreciation. It should be noted, however, that land is not exempt from depreciation, and structures are not exempt from appreciation. Land and structures may either appreciate or depreciate. Federal and state laws govern the use and definition of depreciation.

The generalizations presented here are intended to introduce the concepts and methods used in calculating depreciation. They are not intended as substitutes for any specific laws and regulations applicable to a particular parcel of real estate. Legal counsel should be sought for details of specific state and federal laws. Depreciation has many specific meanings dependent on the application for which it is being used. Depreciation is often used in taxes, accounting, and appraisals.

Depreciation in Taxes

Individuals and businesses use depreciation as a deduction on state and federal income taxes. State and federal tax laws govern the length and terms of tax depreciation. In real estate, the tax deduction is applicable to buildings and improvements, but not land. In business, some qualifying personal property may be depreciated. This type of depreciation allows individuals and businesses to recover the cost of an asset's depreciation. The depreciated value, also known as the book value, is different than an asset's market value. Market value is the amount a willing buyer and willing seller would agree on with neither party under compulsion to buy or sell. Inflation provides that a typical building will have a market value that far exceeds the depreciated value. Consequently, when a building is sold for more than the depreciated value, the excess amount is taxable under certain tax laws.

Depreciation in Accounting

Depreciation is a bookkeeping function in accounting that is used in determining a business's profit and loss. Depreciation is treated as an expense though no real expenses are actually incurred. The economic life of the asset, also known as the useful life of an asset, is used as the basis for depreciation. The economic or useful life is the period of time for which an asset is expected to provide an economic benefit.

Depreciation is not dependent on how long an asset is held, and it has no relationship to payment for an asset. Payment may be in cash, or it may be made in installments with a loan. In the latter, payment is dependent on any loan amount and the terms and interest applied to the loan. Depreciation is the process of spreading the cost of an asset over the period of its useful life. If payment is made within one year, the full purchase price does not become an expense during that year. Only a portion of the price is counted as an expense during the first year, and a portion is then counted for each successive year throughout the useful life of the asset.

The book value of an asset is the cost minus any depreciation of the asset. As such, the book value indicates how much of the asset's cost has not yet been written off as a depreciated expense. The amount of depreciation taken for an asset is often shown in an account called the Reserve for Depreciation. The original cost of an asset should be equal to the sum of the book value and the Reserve for Depreciation.

Depreciation in Appraisals

An appraisal is an estimate or opinion of value determined by a highly skilled professional. An appraisal may be made for real estate or anything considered of value, such as jewelry, furs, automobiles, antiques, and any number of other things. An appraisal is not an exact value but is subject to the competency, integrity, and skill of the particular individual making the appraisal. Most real estate appraisals are provided in the form of a written report, which includes a description of the property, relevant data, and information concerning the property and an analysis of that data.

The value of property in a free market is thought to define the power of a property to command other properties in exchange. In other words, the value of property is relative to the value of other properties. This value may be changed and influenced by many differing factors, such as utility, necessity, sentiment, and the law of supply and demand. Nothing is thought to have value without use. As such, the ability to make use of a property influences the opinion of its value.

Most appraisals are based on market value, which considers not only the present value (or use) of a property but also future benefit from its use. Market value is oftentimes confused with market price. However, these are two different concepts. Market price is the actual price that is paid for a property. Under certain market conditions, it is possible for the market price of a property to be either higher or lower than its market value. Market value is the price at which a willing seller would sell and which a willing buyer would buy, with neither party being under any type of compulsion to buy or sell. This assumes that both parties are informed as to the state of the property and the state of market and that reasonable time allowances are made for market exposure. Many factors contribute the value or lack of value for a property. Influences may be political, economic, or social within a particular community or neighborhood. It has been said that market price is what you pay, and market value is what you get.

Depreciation in appraisals measures the amount by which property value diminishes as a result of physical wasting. Depreciation is used in appraising property using the cost approach method of appraisals. This method assumes that the reproduction cost of a property is its upper limit of value and that any newly constructed building has an advantage over any existing building. The appraiser must therefore determine the disadvantages of existing structures in comparison to new structures and make allowances for such disadvantages. This allowance is what is known as depreciation. This type of depreciation may take on one of three forms: physical deterioration, economic obsolescence, or functional obsolescence. Physical deterioration results from the physical wear and tear of a property. Physical deterioration is easy to identify and is readily seen. Economic obsolesce results from factors outside the property. Social change and other factors within the community have the effect of making the structure less desirable for use. Functional obsolesce is the result of outdated functions within the structure. Such things as the layout, design, or style of a structure or its structural components are outdated as compared to newly constructed properties that serve the same function.

The value of a property is then determined as follows:

- Estimate the value of the land as if were vacant.

- Estimate the current cost of reproducing all improvements to the land.

- Estimate and deduct the depreciation from all causes.

Add the estimated value of the land and the depreciated value of any improvements.

Methods of Depreciation

All assets have a useful or economic life for which the asset is expected to provide an economic benefit. Depreciation is the method of spreading the cost of an asset over the period of its useful life. Depreciation is not affected by how an asset was bought or paid for. There are four primary methods of calculating depreciation: straight line, sinking fund, constant percentage, and sum of digits.

Straight Line Depreciation

The straight-line method of depreciation is probably the most simplistic, most widely used method since it requires only knowledge of arithmetic. The straight-line method allows an equal amount of depreciation to be deducted on an annual basis for a specific period of time. The straight-line method is based on net cost, which is the difference between the actual cost and the estimated salvage value of an asset or the cost to reproduce or replace an asset. There are five component variables that are used:

C = original cost
S = salvage value
n = estimated life (in years)
R = the annual depreciation expense
B = base cost to reproduce or replace

The annual straight-line depreciation expense is calculated as the difference between the cost and salvage value divided by the estimated life or the cost to reproduce or replace as follows:

$$R = \frac{C - S}{n}$$

or

$$R = \frac{B}{n}$$

A depreciated asset has a book value, which is the cost C minus any depreciation taken. The amount of depreciation taken at any given time is called the depreciation reserve. The amount included in a depreciation reserve is equal to the annual depreciation R at the end of k periods. As such, the book value at the end of a period is calculated as:

$$BV_k = C - kR$$

and the cost of the asset is:

$$C = BV_k + kR$$

A depreciation schedule is used to show the depreciation of an asset. The depreciation schedule of an asset indicates its cost, annual depreciation, book value, and any amount included in the depreciation reserve.

Example:

An asset cost $20,000 and has an expected life of 8 years and a salvage value of $1,500. The annual straight-line depreciation is calculated as follows:

$$C = \$20,000$$
$$S = \$1,500$$
$$n = 8$$
$$R = (C - S) \div n$$
$$- (20,000 - 1,500) \div 8$$
$$= 1,8500 \div 8$$
$$= \$2,312.5$$

The depreciation table is constructed as follows:

End of Year	Annual Depreciation	Reserve for Depreciation	Book Value
0			$20,000
1	$2,312.5	$2,312.5	$17,687.50
2	$2,312.5	$4,625.00	$15,375.00
3	$2,312.5	$6,937.50	$13,062.50
4	$2,312.5	$9,250.00	$10,750.00
5	$2,312.5	$11,562.50	$8,437.50
6	$2,312.5	$13,875.00	$6,125.00
7	$2,312.5	$16,187.50	$3,812.50
8	$2,312.5	$18,500.00	$1,500.00
Total	$18,500.00		

The amount of annual depreciation is added to the reserve for depreciation each year. The book value is initially equal to the cost of the asset and is reduced by the annual depreciation each year.

The computations above provide an estimate of annual depreciation. When accrued depreciation is sought, the computation includes an asset's effective age. Let e = effective age of an asset, then:

$$\text{Accrued Depreciation} = \text{annual depreciation} * \text{effective age}$$
$$= R * e$$

Example 1:

After 6 years, a newly constructed house has an estimated value of $21,250, depreciated at 2(½)% annually. The original value of the house is calculated as follows:

$$\text{Annual depreciation expense} = 0.25\%$$
$$\text{Effective age} = 6 \text{ years}$$
$$\text{Accrued depreciation} = .025\% * 6$$
$$= 0.15\%$$

The original value is:

$$\$21,250 \div 0.85$$
$$= \$25,000$$

Example 2:

A lot and structure were purchases for $112,000, 14 years ago. The land value is $32,000. The economic life structure is 40 years, and it is depreciated using the straight-line method of depreciation. The present worth of the property is calculated as follows:

The value of the structures = total value – the value of the land.

$$= \$112,000 - \$32,000$$
$$= \$80,000$$

The economic life of the structures = $(40 - 14)/40 = 26/40$ yrs.

The depreciated value of the structures:

Depreciation = value of structures * economic life of structure
$80,000 * (26/40) = $52,000

The present worth of the property (land and the structures) is $32,000 + $52,000 = $84,000.

Sinking Fund Method of Depreciation

The sinking fund method of depreciation is rarely used in practice, though some public utilities have made use of the procedure, but it is used primarily for analytical estimations of the value of an asset.

A depreciation reserve may be thought of as a fund created to replace an asset, though, in reality, no such fund exits. If such a fund did exist it would be analogous to a sinking fund on which interest is earned at a constant rate. The periodic contribution to the fund would come from two sources. The first source is from the annual periodic charge, and the second source is the accumulating interest on the amount in the fund. As such, the value of the annual contribution would increase each year because the interest income from the fund increases as the size of the fund increases. The annual charge would be the partial payment necessary to accumulate to the value of an asset at maturity, and the periodic charge would be calculated as follows:

$$R = (C - S) * (1 \div S_{n|i})$$

The book value would be calculated as:

$$BV_k = C - (R * S_{k|i})$$
and the cost of the asset would be:
$$C = BV_k + (R * S_{k|i})$$

Example:

A public utility constructs a power line at a cost of $100,000. The line is expected to need replacement in 20 years but by a more costly type of construction. The present line has no salvage value. The sinking fund method is used to determine the annual charge for depreciation, assuming a 6% interest rate. The depreciation charge and book value at the end of the fifth year is calculated as follows:

Let:
$$C = \$100,000$$
$$S = 0$$
$$k = 20 \text{ years}$$
$$i = 6\%$$
$$n = 5$$

$$R = (C - S) * (1 \div S_{n|i})$$
$$R = (100,000 - 0) * (1 \div S_{20|6\%})$$
$$= 100,000 * 0.0271846$$
$$= \$2,718.46$$

$$BV_5 = C - (R * S_{k|i})$$
$$= 100,000 - (2718.46 * S_{5|6\%})$$
$$= 100,000 - (2718.46 * 5.63709296)$$
$$= 100,000 - 15,324.21$$
$$= \$84,675.79$$

End of Year	Annual Depreciation	Interest Earned on Sinking Fund	Amount Added to Sinking Fund	Amount in Sinking Fund	Book Value
0					$100,000
1	$2,718.46	0	$2,718.46	$2,718.46	$97,281.54
2	$2,718.46	$163.11	$2,881.57	$5,600.03	$94,399.97
3	$2,718.46	$336.00	$3,054.46	$8,654.49	$91,345.51
4	$2,718.46	$519.27	$3,237.73	$11,892.22	$88,107.78
5	$2,718.46	$713.53	$3,431.99	$15,324.21	$84,675.79

Constant Percentage or Declining Balance Method of Depreciation

The constant percentage method of computing depreciation is based on the assumption that depreciation is measured as a fixed rate of the book value of an asset. As the book value decreases throughout the asset's useful life, so too does depreciation. The book value at the end of the first year is $C*r$ and the book value at the end of k years is calculated as follows:

$$BV_k = C(1 - r)^k$$

The salvage value S at the end of an asset's useful life is calculated as follows:

$$S = C(1 - R)^n,$$
$$\text{where } S > 0$$
$$\text{and}$$
$$C = S \div (1 - R)^n$$

S must be greater than zero because it is impossible to depreciate an asset to zero by taking a constant percentage of the book value as the deduction for depreciation.

Example:

A machine cost $750 and has an estimated life of 4 years and a salvage value of $150. The constant percentage depreciation is computed as follows:

$$C = 750$$
$$S = 150$$
$$n = 4$$

$$\text{Since } S = C(1 - R)^n, \text{ then}$$
$$R = 1 - \text{antilog} \ [(\log S - \log C) \div n]$$
$$= 1 - \text{antilog} \ [(\log 150 - \log 750) \div 4]$$

$$= 1 - \text{antilog} \left[(2.1760912599 - 2.875061263) \div 4 \right]$$
$$= 1 - \text{antilog } 0.174742501$$
$$= 1 - 0.668740305$$
$$= 0.3313259695$$
$$= 33.126\%$$

Sum of the Digits Method of Computing Depreciation

The sum of the digits method of computing depreciation is similar to the constant percentage method in that it results in a higher depreciation during the early years of computation. The sum of digits method requires that the figures used to represent successive years of an asset's estimated life be added. If an asset has an estimated life of three years, the sum of the digits is $1 + 2 + 3 = 6$. This sum is then used as the denominator in the computation of the fractional portion of an asset's value to be depreciated each year. The numerator is the remaining life of the asset in years. The computation of the fractional amount of depreciation in the first year for an asset that cost $5,000 and has a useful life of 3 years is $3 \div 6 * \$5,000 = \$2,500$. In the second year, the computation is $2 \div 6 * \$5,000 = \$1,666.67$ and in the third year, the computation is $1 \div 6(\$5,000) = \$833.33$.

REAL ESTATE COMPENSATION AND COMMISSION

The compensation received in the form of commission on the sale, purchase, lease, rent, or transfer of real estate is shared between the real estate broker and any real estate salespersons involved in the particular transaction. A real estate broker is oftentimes confused with a real estate salesperson. It must be understood that a real estate salesperson is an employee of a real estate broker. Certain restrictions limit the activities of the salesperson and distinguish him or her from the broker. Licensing laws dictate that a broker is responsible for policy making and the individual subjected to such policy is the salesperson. Real estate transactions require the responsibility to collect commissions, provide receipts of deposits, and engage in advertisement. Any salesperson that takes on these responsibilities without the permission or approval of a broker is in violation of the licensing laws.

Real Estate Broker

The real estate broker is an entrepreneur who engages in activities to bring together those who have real estate to be marketed and those who have a need for real estate. The real estate broker serves as a third party in buying and selling transactions and receives compensation in the form of a commission for a successful transaction. The real estate broker may represent either the buyer or seller, but does not ordinarily represent both parties of a transaction. In most instances, the real estate broker represents the seller. A licensed real estate broker may hire other individuals as real estate salespersons. The salesperson staff allows the real estate broker to expand the perimeters of the business by providing additional staff to handle transactions with more than one person or properties at the same time. The hired salesperson must be an individual who holds a state license for real estate sales. The hired salesperson cannot be a corporation or other business entity. The relationship between a real estate broker and a real estate salesperson is that of employer and employee, respectively.

Real Estate Salesperson

A real estate salesperson is a person employed by a licensed real estate broker to buy, sell, rent, lease, or exchange real estate for others. The real estate salesperson acts and receives compensation under the direction and guidance of the employing real estate broker. The salesperson's license provides that the salesperson operates as an extension of the broker's physical facilities. It is through the broker's salespersons that a broker is able to deal concurrently with multiple persons and properties. Though, for tax purposes, many brokers contract work with their salespersons as independent contractors, the employer-employee relationship makes the broker responsible for the acts of his or her salespersons.

The real estate salesperson always acts as an agent for the employing broker, not in an individual capacity. Contracts and agreements that have been negotiated by the salesperson are drawn in the name of the broker and must bear the broker's signature in order to be considered valid. Any subsequent legal actions resulting from such agreements will have the broker as the named party to the action with the salesperson having only an incidental role as the broker's employee.

Most real estate salespersons receive compensation for their work in the form of a percentage of the total commission paid to his or her real estate broker for the broker's involvement in a particular transaction. The exact percentage is as defined by a contractual agreement between the broker and the salesperson. That contractual agreement may have many variables that affect the determination of the salesperson's percentage of commission. As an example, the salesperson that lists a property but does not sell the property may receive a portion of any commission received from the sale during the term of the salesperson's listing, irrespective of who was responsible for making the sale. The salesperson that made the sale would also receive a portion of the commission for having brought about the sale.

Brokerage Cycle for Property Sales

In the sale of real estate, the broker may act on behalf of the buyer or seller. The real estate brokerage cycle for property sales involves four primary steps: listing, agreement of sale, financing, and title closing or escrow.

- The listing of a property for sale by a real estate brokerage firm is accomplished by means of an agency contract, which is called a listing in the vernacular of the trade. The broker and owner complete and provide signature to an agency agreement.

- After the listing is secured, the broker seeks a purchaser, and when one is found, an agreement of sale is drawn between the purchaser and seller. In many instances this agreement is in the form of a deposit receipt with the actual sales contract drawn at a later date.

- The financing of the sale requires the completion of a credit application and an appraisal of the property. It may also be necessary to arrange a survey of the property and a property inspection.

- After a loan is approved, the title closing or escrow phase begins. This requires the preparation of a deed to the property, mortgages or deeds of trust, notes, bonds for the repayment of the loan, title insurance, hazard insurance, and the recording of instruments.

MORTGAGES

The mathematics of mortgages includes computations of the down payment, loan amount, discount points, property taxes, and the total monthly mortgage payment. Total monthly mortgage payments typically include the mortgage principal, interest, property taxes, and homeowners insurance. Collectively, these components of a monthly mortgage payment are known as PITI. In establishing a particular mortgage loan, a comparison of different loans, including fixed rate and adjustable rate mortgage plans, may be considered.

The relationship between the amount of borrowed money and the appraised value of a property is known as the loan to value ratio (LTV or L/V). The LTV ratio indicates the percent of the purchase price or appraised value that the lender loans the borrower. This ratio is a measure of the financial risk associated with borrowing and lending money. The loan to value ratio is computed as follows:

$$\text{Loan to value ratio} = \text{loan amount} \div \text{purchase price or appraised value}$$

Down Payments

The amount of down payment required to secure a mortgage loan is dependent on the type of financing. There are three primary types of mortgage financing: FHA, VA, and conventional financing. FHA and VA are federally insured mortgage loans.

FHA Down Payments

The down payment required for an FHA mortgage is governed by amendment to the National Housing Act, known as the FHA Down Payment Simplification Act of 2002. The amendment is designed to permanently simplify the down payment requirements for FHA-insured mortgages for single-family home buyers. The maximum amount of an FHA residential mortgage loan is based on a fixed percentage of the sale price or appraised value of the property, whichever is less. The FHA has established two types of percentages: one for low closing cost states and the other for high closing cost states. Most states are considered high closing cost states. The percentages specified for high closing cost states are as follows:

Percentage	Sale Price or Appraised Value (whichever is less)
98.75%	Equal to or less than $50,000
97.75%	More than $50,000

FHA-insured loans are provided in even increments of $50.

VA Down Payments

VA mortgage loans are only available to veterans, spouses of veterans, and active duty military personnel. The VA establishes loan guarantee limits for VA mortgage loans, known as the VA loan guarantee or the maximum entitlement. The current entitlement is $89,912. The granting of the loan is preceded by the issuing of a certificate of eligibility that indicates the amount of entitlement available to the borrower. This entitlement is based on the loan amount as follows:

Loan amount	Guaranteed Amount
0 to $45,000	50% of the loan amount
$45,001 to $144,000	Minimum of $22,500 and maximum of up to 40% of the loan, up to $36,000
More than $144,000	Up to $89,912 or 25% of the loan amount

Since the maximum loan guarantee is $89,912 or 25% of the loan amount, the maximum loan amount, with no down payment, is calculated as $89,912 * 4 = $359,650. However, no maximum loan amount is actually established for VA mortgage loans. Limitations stipulate that the loan cannot exceed the appraised value of the property as determined by a VA approved appraiser and as stated in the Certificate of Reasonable Value (CRV). Another limitation is that the borrower's income and ability to pay the total monthly mortgage payment must be inclusive of all costs of PITI. Also, the borrower's total monthly obligation may not exceed 41% of the borrower's monthly gross income. Total monthly obligations include PITI and other long-term debts. Long-term debts are debts that cannot be paid off within ten months.

Recipients of VA mortgage loans are required to pay a funding fee or user's fee to defray the government's cost of foreclosure. The funding fee is assessed as a percentage of the mortgage amount, depending on how many times the borrower has made use of the benefit. The funding fee is waived for veterans with service related disabilities. All other eligible borrowers may finance the funding fee by adding it to the loan amount, which may increase the maximum loan amount. However, the funding fee must not increase the maximum loan amount beyond $359,650. As an alternative to financing, the funding fee may be included in the closing costs.

Conventional Down Payments

Conventional mortgage loans are generally acquired at 50 to 90% of the total value of a property. Private mortgage insurance (PMI) provides a method of allowing a buyer to purchase property with a down payment as little as 3% of the sale price or appraised value of the property, whichever is lowest. However, most conventional mortgage loans generally require a larger down payment than government sponsored mortgage loans. Most lenders require the borrower to acquire PMI when more than 80% of the value of the property is borrowed.

Conventional mortgage loan down payments are always required as a percentage of the selling price. The amount of such a down payment is computed as follows:

amount of down payment = selling price * percent required

Mortgage Loan Amounts

Mortgage loan amounts include the principal and interest of mortgage payments, but it also includes property tax and hazard insurance costs. Portions of a monthly mortgage payment are allocated to the principal amount of the funds borrowed, the interest applied, a property tax, and hazard insurance. The payment includes principal and interest at the contractual rate, as well as $^1/_{12}$ of the annual property tax and $^1/_{12}$ of the annual hazard insurance premium. These four payment amounts are collectively referred to as a PITI (principal, interest, tax, and insurance) payment.

Discount Points

Mortgage lenders charge points as an interest discount factor. Traditionally, the system of discount points was used to make the lower interest rates charged for federally sponsored mortgage loans competitive with the higher interest rates charged for conventional mortgage loans. Demand, inflation, and other money market conditions have since caused lenders to assess points on all types of mortgage loans. Discount points are charged as an up front fee to increase the lender's yield without having to increase the interest rate of the mortgage. Discount points are assessed based on the loan amount.

Lenders use computer software or established tables to determine the amount of discount points to charge a borrower. As an estimate, each discount point paid to the lender increases the lender's effective yield by about $^1/_8$ of 1% or 0.00125. This computation provides an estimate of the lender's effective yield and the borrower's cost. As such, each discount point charged by the lender adds $^1/_8$% to the cost of the original mortgage loan interest rate. The computation is deigned to estimate the mortgage interest rate cost as an annual percentage rate, not a dollar amount. The contractual mortgage interest rate will not change. To determine the actual dollar cost of discount points, each discount point is equated to 1% of the mortgage balance. To find the dollar amount of the discount being charged, the mortgage loan amount is multiplied by the appropriate discount percent. When a lender indicates that a mortgage is "going at" some value, for example 99, the lender is implying that 1 discount point is applied to the mortgage.

Property Tax

The assessment of property taxes provides local governments with revenue needed to fund public services. Property taxes are levied on an ad valorem basis, or they are based on the value of a property. The term ad valorem means according to value. As such, ad valorem taxes provide a method of requiring property owners to share the cost of government services in proportion to the value of their property. The local appraiser or tax assessor is responsible for assessing a fair and reasonable value of properties using one of three approaches to determining property value: the sales comparison approach, the cost depreciation approach, or the income approach. The assessed value of a property differs from the market value of a property since the assessed value is established for the purpose of computing property taxes.

Taxable Value

The taxable value of property is the assessment value minus any applicable exemptions to the property tax. Many states allow an exemption from property taxes for homestead properties, persons with disabilities, and other considerations of the state. A homestead property is a single primary residence. A homestead property exemption is intended to make property taxes progressive, reducing the property burden on low income and fixed income residents. The exemption is usually calculated as a fixed monetary amount, such as the first $50,000 of the property's assessed value. The remaining value of the property is taxed at the normal rate of property tax.

The taxable value is the amount by which a rate is applied to arrive at the amount of property tax to be paid. The property tax rate is usually expressed in mills rather than as a percent. A mill is 1/1000 of a dollar. As such, 35% = .035% = 35 mills. To convert from decimal notation to mills, the decimal point is moved three places to the right, which is the same as multiplying the decimal value by 1,000. Conversely, to convert from millage to a decimal value, the decimal point is moved three places to the left, which is equivalent to dividing the millage value by 1,000. Tax rates may be expressed in a variety ways, including the following

- 21 mills per $1 of assessed valuation

- $.021 per $1 of assessed valuation

- $2.10 per $100 of assessed valuation

- $21 per $,1000 of assessed valuation

The decimal notation is always specified to three digits.

Assessment

Governments assess taxes on the taxable value of a property. If no exemptions apply to the property, the taxable value and the assessed value are the same. If exemptions are applicable to a property, the exemption is subtracted from the assessed value to determine a taxable value. The dollar amount of property taxes is then computed from multiplying the taxable value by the tax rate. The tax assessed on real estate is determined by the market value in which the parcel is located and the tax rate established by the local government. The tax is assessed as dollars or cents per hundred or per thousand dollars of assessment. The tax rate is expressed in mills per dollar of the assessed value. A table of tax rates for the largest cities in each state is provided at **www.census.gov/compendia/statab/tables/07s0437. xls** and is provided in Appendix 3.

Assessed value = market value * assessment ratio
Annual tax = assessed value * tax rate

Example:

The property tax assessment of a property in Baltimore City is $75,000. The table in Appendix 3 shows that Baltimore uses a 2.46% tax rate. The annual tax is calculated as follows:

$75,000 * .0246 = $1,845

Equalization

In some jurisdictions, assessed property values are adjusted to make them comparable to values in surrounding jurisdictions. An equalization factor is used as determined by the responsible tax assessor's office. The annual property tax when equalization is in effect is computed as:

Annual tax = assessed value * equalization factor * tax rate

Special Assessments

Special assessments are a one-time tax on properties to assist with the funding of certain types of improvements to the property, such as street paving, sidewalk repair, and so on.

Example:

The city will pay 34% of the cost to construct a new alleyway, which is $47 per front foot. Properties that adjoin the alley have a standard 50 front feet. The cost to residents is computed as follows:

Total cost for each property
50 front feet * $47 per front foot = $2,350

City's share of the cost for each property
0.34 * $2,350 = $799

Each resident's share of the cost
(1 − 0.34) * $2,350 = $1,551

State Documentary Stamp Tax on Deeds

The term documentary implies the intent to imprint or place tax stamps on documents, such as deeds to property. The tax stamp may be assessed as a percentage of the purchase price. This tax is based on the total purchase price of a property. There is no consideration for how the funds are acquired to make the purchase.

Community Millage Rate

Local governments use the revenue from property taxes to fund the expenses of the community, such as fire protection and emergency medial services. Revenue is also received from other sources, such as sales tax, parking tickets, and other local charges. The amount of revenue available from all properties in a local community is calculated as the total of all assessed property values minus all applicable local exemptions. Not only are homestead properties eligible for property tax exemptions, but also government buildings, properties owned by churches, and nonprofit organizations. The millage rate that must be charged by local governments to meet its budgetary needs is a function of the assessed value of properties and the exemptions allowed for properties.

Millage rate = property tax revenue ÷ (total assessed values
– applicable exemptions)

Property Tax Penalties

Local governments impose a penalty for the failure to pay assessed property taxes within a timely manner. The penalty is assessed on delinquencies at interest as established by tax laws of the local government. The penalty is assessed per month per amount of delinquency. When the property owner fails to pay delinquent property taxes, the property may be offered for sale at a tax sale or a private sale. In most states, the delinquent owner is allowed a specified period of time to redeem the property before the property actually transfers ownership. Additional penalties and interest are usually added until such time as the property is redeemed.

Mortgage Tax

In some states, a tax is assessed when there is an establishment of debt on a property. A new mortgage or assumption of an existing mortgage are the two common methods of establishing debt on a property. Some states require that two separate taxes be assessed on the establishment of mortgages and other instruments associated with debts, such as promissory notes and deeds of trust. The two taxes that may be assessed on a newly established mortgage note are known as the intangible tax and the documentary stamp tax on a note. An intangible state tax is a one-time tax paid on new mortgages. This tax is usually assessed as a percentage of the newly established debt on the property. The documentary stamp tax on a note is also a one-time tax that is included as part of a mortgage package. This tax is due on execution of a mortgage note and is assessed as a fractional portion of the face value of the note.

In the states that assess taxes on mortgages, every real estate transaction involving new financing reflects the cost of mortgage taxes. When financing involves an assumption of an existing mortgage, which obligates a buyer to assume liability for a debt, the note that is executed is subject to a documentary stamp tax. If there are no changes in the property that secures the assumed loan, a new mortgage is not created, and as such, no intangible taxes are assessed.

The table in Appendix 2 lists the real estate transfer rates for each state as documented by the Federation of Tax Administrators.

Example:

An investor purchased a property in Maryland in 2004 for $207,000. The property is located in a jurisdiction that taxes at the highest rate. The total of all taxes paid by the investor are computed as follows:

Maryland assesses the following taxes on the transfer of property:

1. Transfer tax:	Up to 0.5% of the purchase price
2. Local deed recordation tax:	$2.20 to $5 per $500 of value
3. Local transfer tax:	Up to 1.5% of the purchase price

The transfer tax is computed as:
.005 * 207,000 = $1,035
The local deed recordation tax is computed as:
$207,000 ÷ 500 = 414 taxable units
414 * $5 = $2,070
The local transfer tax is computed as:
.015 * $207,000 = $3,105
The total tax is:
$1,035 + $2,070 + $3,105 = $6,210

Debt Ratios

Debt ratio is a measure of the percentage of monthly income that is applied to monthly long-term debt obligations, which are debts that cannot be paid within ten months. Lenders consider debt ratios when qualifying potential borrowers for a mortgage loan or mortgage loan program. Different loan programs establish differing guidelines regarding debt ratios. Conventional mortgage loans have lower debt ratio requirements than government sponsored VA and FHA mortgage loans. This allows more potential home buyers to qualify for government loan programs. There are actually two types of debt ratio: a housing expense debt ratio and a total obligation debt ratio.

A housing expense debt ratio measures the percentage of monthly income that is applied to monthly house payments. House payments are inclusive of all the elements of PITI. The housing expense ratio is calculated as follows:

Housing expense ratio = PITI ÷ monthly gross income

The total obligation debt ratio is an extension of the housing expense ratio since it includes PITI, as well as other non-housing long-term debt obligations (PITIO).

Total obligation expense ratio = PITIO ÷ monthly gross income

Table 5: Debt Ratios for Mortgage		
	Debt Ratios	
	Housing Expense Ratio	Total Monthly Obligations Ratio
FHA	29%	41%
VA	Not Used	41%
Conventional	28%	36%

Only the total monthly obligations ratio is used for VA loans. The highest total monthly obligations ratio is for FHA and VA loans.

Types of loans require the least monthly income in relation to monthly debts.

Example:

A home buyer with a gross income of $80,000 per year expects to make mortgage payments of $1,082.76 per month with taxes of $632 per year and insurance of $287 per year. The home buyer also has an outstanding student loan payment of $243 per month. The housing expense and total obligation ratios are computed as follows.

Principal and interest are included in the mortgage payment.

Gross monthly income
$$= \$60,000 \div 12$$
$$= \$5,000$$

The monthly PITI
$$= \$1,082.76 + (\$632 \div 12) + (\$287 \div 12)$$
$$= \$1,082.76 + 52.67 + 23.92$$
$$= \$1,159.35$$

The monthly PITIO
$$= \$1,159.35 + \$243$$
$$= \$1,402.35$$

Housing expense ratio
$$= \$1,159.35 \div \$5,000$$
$$= 0.23$$
$$= 23\%$$

Total obligations ratio
$$= \$1,402.35 \div \$5,000$$
$$= 0.28$$
$$= 28\%$$

The home buyer meets the debt ratio requirements for the three primary types of mortgage financing.

Mortgage Amortization

Mortgages usually involve a level-payment plan in which regular and equal payments are made to the lender. The amount of payment towards the interest gradually decreases as the amount of payment towards the principal balance of the debt increases over the life of the mortgage loan. The term amortize means to extinguish or deaden. Amortized mortgages will gradually be extinguished by regular payments.

The amount of payment that is applied toward extinguishing the principal and interest is dependent on the outstanding amount of principal debt, the interest rate charged for the mortgage, and the amount of payment per period. Amortization involves compound interest in which the first payment of principal and interest reduces the balance of interest and principal, and at the same time, interest is applied to the principal balance. The percentage of the original loan amount that is required to be paid each year to pay the annual interest on the outstanding balance and fully amortize the loan over the term of the loan is called a loan constant or mortgage constant. A monthly loan constant is the percentage of the original loan amount that is required to be paid each month.

INCOME PROPERTY VALUATION

An income property is considered to be a stream of income, which is generated by the operation of the property, independent of external factors that allow one to hold title and rights to the property or prolong the life of the property, such as financing, taxes, and capital improvements. When an investor purchases an income property, the investor is in fact purchasing the income stream associated with that property.

In real estate, net income is formally recognized as net operating income (NOI). The NOI of a real estate investment is defined as a property's gross operating income (GOI) minus the operating expenses and any credit loss. Two primary elements used in the valuation of property are the NOI and the capitalization rate, also called the cap rate. The NOI represents the return on investment for the purchase price of an income property, and the capitalization rate represents the rate of that return. If an income property is purchased for $100,000 and the NOI is $1,000, the property has a 10% cap rate. An investor then makes a decision to purchase such a property if the investor is satisfied with the 10% rate of return. The NOI represents an objective measure of income stream, and the required cap rate is a subjective measure of how well an investor expects the invested capital to perform. The determination of NOI is a science based on definition and formula. The determination of cap rate is an art based on external factors, such as market conditions and tax laws.

If interest rates go up, the investor may seek other forms of investment, or it is likely that the investor will maintain an interest in the income property only if the return is higher. Otherwise, the investor would need to acquire the property at a lower cost to receive a higher return. A rise in interest rates is an external event, external to the operation of the property. It has no effect on the NOI. It does affect the rate-of-return or cap rate that a buyer will demand for the property. As such, a change in demand for rates of return impacts the market value of the property.

Cash flow and taxable income are extensions of NOI. Cash flow is actual money. Once the NOI of a property is known, the taxable income and cash flow may be computed. In determining taxable income, only the interest portion of any loan amount is deducted. Any interest earned is added back to income. Depreciation and amortization are also deducted. In purchasing income property, the full cost of the investment cannot be deducted as an investment expense. A portion of the value is depreciated each year until the value of the property is reached. The tax laws regarding real estate provide for physical structures to be treated as depreciable assets but not the land on which such structures are erected. Current tax laws provide for residential income property to be depreciated over 27.5 years, and a nonresidential property to be depreciated over 39 years. The deduction makes use of the half-month convention, which dictates that one-half of the normal amount of depreciation be deducted in the month in which the property was placed in service and one-half in the month the property was sold. Taxable income is also affected by amortization. Amortization, in this sense, is the partial tax deduction for an item that is not allowed as an expense. Points paid on a mortgage loan are typically amortized. Points are paid in one lump sum at the loan closing, and the amount paid is amortized over the life of the loan. If a 360-month income property loan with 3 points is secured for $90,000, the amount of points is calculated as .03 * $90,000 = $2,700. Points totaling $2,700 are paid at closing and an equivalent amount of $7.50 per month = $90 per year may be deducted over the 30-year life of the loan. The interest earned on any bank account established for the property or escrow account required to pay taxes and insurance is also subtracted from the NOI.

Taxable income = NOI – interest payments – any allowable deductions for appreciation and amortization + any interest earned OR
taxable income = NOI – tax deductible expense + non-rental income

Mortgage payments and capital improvements affect the cash flow as soon as they are paid. However, the cost may be depreciated over 27.5 or 39 years. Any interest earned on accounts of the property adds to cash flows.

Cash flow = NOI – everything spent, but not accounted for
in NOI + non-rental income

RETURN ON INCOME PROPERTY

An investment in income property precludes that one will collect income from the property, primarily in the form of rent, and use that amount to pay operating expenses and debts against the property and to have a surplus or profit that can be sheltered from excess taxes. At some point, the income producing property may also be sold for profit. As such, an investment in income producing properties requires knowledge of the four basic forms of return: appreciation, amortization, cash flow, and tax shelters.

Though there are many schemes advertised as "no money down," chances are that something will have to be invested because if nothing is invested, there is no investment. When 100% of an income property is financed, the debt service associated with this type of financing is likely to cause a negative cash flow. Rather than having to pay money up front, money is needed every month to make up the difference between cash inflow and outflow. The cost of this type of high risk financing is usually high with higher rates and short repayment terms. Also, the acceptance of this type of financing may be an indication of a problem property.

The income and expenses associated with an income property should be documented in an annual property operating data (APOD) statement or some similar type of documentation. An APOD statement is the real estate equivalent of the accountant's income-and-expense statement. The statements are often used interchangeably. An APOD statement provides the data necessary for evaluating the performance of a property and also indicates existing or potential problems with the property. Operating expenses include the costs necessary to keep the property in a condition to produce income. Operating expenses may include the costs of repairs, utilities, insurance, and taxes. However, mortgage payments, depreciation, and capital improvements are not considered operating expenses.

The annual rent received from all units of an income property is called the gross scheduled income of the property. The gross scheduled income includes rent from occupied units, as well as potential rent from any vacant units. A vacancy allowance is used to estimate the potential income from vacancies. Vacancy allowance is expressed as a percent of gross scheduled income, and it represents lost income. A vacancy allowance may also be referred to as a "vacancy and credit loss" when it includes the loss due to uncollectible rent. The measure of gross scheduled income minus any vacancy allowance is called the gross operating income (GOI). The GOI is also referred to as the effective gross income. It represents the actual amount of rent that is received. The measure of gross scheduled income minus any operating expense is called the net operating income (NOI). The NOI represents rental income after any expenses and vacancy allowances are deducted. Mortgage payments and capital expenditures are not included in the calculation of NOI.

Example:

A 10-unit apartment complex rents units at $740 per month and incurs operating expenses of $6,800 during the year.

This information is used to describe the property as follows:

Gross Scheduled Income:	$740 per month * 12 months * 10 units $740 * 12 * 10 = $88,800
3% Vacancy Allowance:	3% of $88,800 = .03 * $88,800 = $2,664
GOI:	Gross Scheduled Income – Vacancy Allowance $88,800 – $2,664 = $86,136
Operating Expenses:	$6,800
NOI:	Gross Scheduled Income – Operating Expenses $88,800 – $6,800 = $82, 000

The vacancy allowance is 3% of the gross scheduled income. This amount represents an estimate that is based on knowledge of market conditions of comparable properties in the same area. In the absence of such data, a vacancy allowance is usually chosen in the range of 3 to 6%, except when the property is being leased for the first time. In this case, vacancies will be much higher, and the allowance should represent a greater portion of the gross scheduled income. It should be noted that a property that has a history of few or no vacancies is likely to have charged rent that is less than market rates or is not charging enough rent.

Not all investments in income properties are based on the potential income of the property. Some investors are more interested in the benefit of selling such properties. For a successful investment that has produced a profit and appreciated in value, the sale of the property will be profitable. As an additional benefit, the proceeds from the sale may be taxed as a capital gain, which provides for a lower tax rate than the tax on ordinary income.

Cash Flow

Cash flow is a measure of a property's cash inflows minus all the cash outflows during a specified period of time. Cash inflows are included in the calculation of cash flow whether or not they fall into the category of taxable income. Likewise, cash outflows are included whether or not they are tax deductible. As an example, only the interest portion of mortgage payments is tax deductible, but the total mortgage payment is included in the calculation of cash flow. Cash inflows may include such incoming cash as rent, proceeds from loans, and interest on bank accounts of the investment. Outflows may include capital additions, debt payments, and operating expenses. Cash flow may be computed before or after income tax liabilities of the property have been included.

The calculation of cash flow requires an application of compound interest. As with any application of compound interest, four variables must be considered. They include the following:

- PV = the initial dollar amount or present value

- FV = the final compounded amount, which is the amount to which the initial dollar amount grows after all interest has been applied during the compounding period
- i = the periodic interest rate
- N = the number of compounding periods

The calculation for PV is:

$$PV = \frac{FV}{(1 + i)^N}$$

Also, the number of periods is calculated as :

$$N = \frac{\log (FV/PV)}{\log (1 + i)}$$

The calculation for N requires the use of logarithms, but may be more easily calculated with a calculator or an electronic spreadsheet, such as Excel, which has built-in functions to handle such complex mathematical operations. The present value (PV) of future cash flow is used to determine the worth of cash in today's dollars.

Cash flow is a measure of the incoming cash and the outgoing cash. A positive cash flow is always desirable, but in the business of income property, cash flow will always be greater in some years than in others. When an income property is sold, the proceeds from the sale are also considered part of the cash flow. The time value of money is an important consideration when valuating the cash flow of income property. Cash received sooner is more valuable since it is available to reinvest. The longer it takes to receive cash, the less it has the potential to earn. A dollar to be received in ten years has less value than a dollar held today since the dollar is expected to lose buying power over time. In the business of investments, one must be able to calculate the loss in value caused by future dollar investments.

Discounting is one method of calculating the loss of value from future dollar investments. With income properties, some return on investment is expected each year, along with an additional return on investment when the property is sold. Each of these returns has its own timing and requires its own calculation of discount. The discount is applied to the individual years, and the amounts are summed to arrive at a discount for the total investment.

Example:

A rental property is acquired for $100,000. The following cash flows are acquired from a rental property for the past five years. The cash flow represents the amount remaining after all operating expenses are paid and all debts are satisfied. Similar properties in the area with similar risk earn a return of 10% annually, and it is anticipated that this particular property will also earn 10%. As such, the discount on future returns is established at no less than 10%. After the five years, the property is sold for $150,000, which is included in the fifth year of cash flow. The investment is profitable if the PV of the down payment exceeds the down payment.

Year	Cash Flow
1	10,500
2	11,000
3	11,500
4	12,000
5	162,500

The individual PV associated with each cash flow is as follows:

Year 1: $10,500 is discounted 1 year at 10%. The PV is:

$$PV = FV \div (1 + i)^N$$
$$= \$10,500 \div (1 + .10)$$
$$= \$10500 \div 1.1$$
$$= \$9,545.45$$

Year 2: $11,000 is discounted 2 years at 10%. The PV is:

$$PV = FV \div (1 + i)^N$$
$$= \$11,000 \div (1 + .10)^2$$
$$= \$11000 \div 1.21$$
$$= \$9,090.91$$

Year 3: $11,500 is discounted 3 years at 10%. The PV is:

$$PV = FV \div (1 + i)^N$$
$$= \$11,500 \div (1 + .10)^3$$
$$= \$11,500 \div 1.331$$
$$= \$8,640.12$$

Year 4: $12,000 is discounted 4 years at 10%. The PV is:

$$PV = FV \div (1 + i)^N$$
$$= \$12,000 \div (1 + .10)^4$$
$$= \$12,000 \div 1.4641$$
$$= \$8,196.16$$

Year 5: $162,500 is discounted 5 years at 10%. The PV is:

$$PV = FV \div (1 + i)^N$$
$$= \$162,500 \div (1 + .10)^5$$
$$= \$162,500 \div 1.61051$$
$$= \$100,899.72$$

The sum of the individual PVs is:

$9,545.45
$9,090.91
$8,640.12
$8,196.16
$100,899.72
$136,372.36

The sum $136,372.36 represents the value today that the property is expected to bring in the future. This sum exceeds the $100,000 needed to acquire the property. As such, the investment is profitable. The difference between the investment amount and the total PV is known as net present value (NPV).

$$NPV = 136{,}372.36 - 100{,}000 = 36{,}372.36$$

Net Present Value

Net present value is the difference between the present value of all future cash flows and the amount of initial investment. If the difference is positive or zero, the rate of return indicated by the discount is equaled or exceed.

$$NPV = PV \text{ of all future cash flows} - \text{initial cash investment}$$

Profitability Index

A profitability index is a measure of investment return that measures the ratio of the present value of all future cash flows and the amount of initial investment. The index is equal to 1 if the present value of cash flows equals the cash investment. This index is useful for comparing two investments that require differing initial investment amounts.

The profitability index of the example above is calculated as

$$\text{Profitability index} = PV \text{ of all future cash flows} \div \text{initial cash investment}$$
$$= \$136{,}372.36 \div \$100{,}000$$
$$= 1.36$$

Cash on Cash Return

A cash on cash return, also called an equity dividend rate, is a measure of the ratio between the cash flow from a property and the initial investment in the property. Cash on cash return is determined on a yearly basis and is often determined before taxes. This measure is often assessed for the first year of ownership since the calculation does not account for the time value of money. However, it can be based on projections for future years. Cash on cash return is not considered a powerful analysis tool for investment property but a handy tool to be used for comparisons with other types of investments.

Cash on cash return = annual cash flow ÷ cash invested

Example:

A property is purchased with a down payment of $10,000. For the first year, the net operating income is $9,000 with a cash flow of $800. The cash on cash return is:

$$\$800 \div \$10,000$$
$$= 0.08$$
$$= 8\%.$$

Internal Rate of Return

The internal rate of return (IRR) is a more widely accepted measure of the rate of return. IRR considers the timing and magnitude of cash flows from an income property. IRR is a measure of the discount rate due to a forecast of future cash flows and the present value of actual cash investments. The computation of IRR is complex and iterative and is best left to some tool of digital computation, such as an Excel. With Excel, the initial investment amount and the projected cash flows may be input to arrive at a value for IRR.

Return on Equity

Return on equity (ROE) is a measure of cash flow and the initial cash investment. There are two calculations for ROE, both based on the measure of cash flow after taxes. In one calculation, equity is simply the initial cash investment in the property. In the other calculation, equity includes the initial cash investment and any additional equity due to amortization of the mortgage or an increase in value of the property. ROE is a percentage, often measured for the first year of ownership.

ROE = cash flow after taxes ÷ initial cash investment

Or

ROE = cash flow after taxes ÷ (resale value – mortgage balance)

Examples:

An investor purchases a property with an $80,000 down payment. In the first year of operation, the property provides a cash flow of $4,000 after taxes. The ROE is:

ROE = cash flow after taxes ÷ initial cash investment

= $4,000 ÷ $80,000

= 0.05

= 5%

The same property is valued at $240,000 at the end of the first year, and there is a mortgage balance of $158,000. The ROE is:

ROE = cash flow after taxes ÷ (resale value – mortgage balance)

ROE = $4,000 ÷ ($240,000 – $158,000)

= $4,000 ÷ $82,000

= .049

= 4.9%

Performance Ratios

Performance ratios are necessary to assist investors in evaluating potential investment opportunities. These ratios range from advanced mathematical models to rules of thumb. Many investors, particularly inexperienced investors, rely on sales of similar properties in evaluating the potential of income property. While doing so is part of the evaluation process, a more comprehensive approach should be taken to evaluate the value of a property, including all facets of a property's income and expenses. This type of evaluation is the only real method of knowing in advance of investing whether an investor is paying too much or getting a good deal.

There are 10 essential performance measurements that may be used to provide this more comprehensive assessment of income property. The ten essential performance measures are as follows:

1	Net Operating Income	NOI
2	Capitalization Rate	Cap Rate
3	Net Income ROI	
4	Cash ROI	Owner's Equity
5	Total ROI	
6	Debt Service Coverage Ratio	DSCR
7	Gross Rent Multiplier	GRM
8	Operating Ratio	OR
9	Break-even Ratio	BER
10	Operating Efficiency Ratio	OER

Ratios are one the most important methods used in measuring the relationships between variables that describe the components of income property. A ratio is a mathematical expression of the relationship between two groups of numbers. As such, ratios provide a gauge for measuring the differences between two or more things. Ratio analysis precludes that value is a relative measure. The value of a property has no meaning by itself. It only has meaning relative to the value of another property, particularly one that is similar. In a typical analysis, the value of a property is considered to be an amount that is equal or less than the fair market value relative to other properties that are similar in design and function.

In the same manner that property value is relative, so too are the performance measurements that capture those values. As an example, capitalization rates and sale price are a function of property value, which are determined, in part, by the location of the property. An investment in a favorable neighborhood would command a lower cap rate, but a higher price than a property in a deteriorating neighborhood. This type of property is more likely to attract buyers who prefer a higher quality asset. Conversely, a property located in a deteriorating neighborhood would command a higher cap rate and lower price. This type of property is more likely to attract buyers seeking a higher yield. Both types of property may coexist in the same metropolitan area, but one is considered to be a better buy than the other.

Return on investment (ROI) is a performance measure ratio that measures how much an investment will make in dollars. Investors need to be able to figure out the return on investment dollars before investing those dollars. ROI is used to measure the effectiveness of a number of real estate assets. It is used to capture the relationship between net income, cash flow, and an asset's total return against investment dollars.

Net Operating Income (NOI)

Net operating income is a measure of income after all operating expenses have been paid. It is also a measure of the amount of income available to service debts of the property. Net operating income is calculated as follows:

NOI = gross income – total operating expenses

Example:

An apartment produces a gross monthly return of $15,000. Annul expenses are $60,000. The NOI is calculated as follows:

$$Gross\ income = \$15,000 * 12$$
$$= \$180,000$$
$$NOI = gross\ income - total\ operating\ expense$$
$$= \$180,000 - \$60,000$$
$$= \$120,000$$

Capitalization Ratio (Cap Rate)

The capitalization ratio, also referred to as cap rate, is a measure of the ratio of net operating income to the sale price of a property. The cap rate is calculated as follows:

$$Cap\ Rate = NOI \div sales\ price$$

The process of converting income to a single value is called capitalization. The cap rate is a measure of that single value. The calculated cap rate is similar to yield in financial instruments, such as certificates of deposit (CD). In the same manner that banks offer CDs with interest that falls within a certain range, dependent on market conditions, properties may be purchased within a range of interest rates. Often CDs are offered in a range of 4 to 6%, and properties are offered for sale in a range of 6 to 10%, depending on market conditions. The stated percentages are not absolute, since market conditions, which include such things as the interest rate environment, tax implications, supply, and demand, vary from state to state.

NOI is used in the calculation of a property's capitalization rate, and it is also used in estimating the approximate sale price of income producing properties.

Example 1:

Apartment buildings in a certain area are experiencing a cap rate of 10%, and it is known that the NOI for a particular building for sale in that area is $350,000. The sale price is estimated as:

$$\text{Sale Price} = \text{NOI} \div \text{cap rate}$$
$$= \$350,000 \div .10$$
$$= \$3,500$$

Example 2:

An apartment building yields $30,000 annually and is placed on the market for $500,000. We want to determine if this is a fair price.

$$\text{NOI} = \$30,000$$
$$\text{Sale Price} = \$500,000$$
$$\text{Cap Rate} = \text{NOI} \div \text{sales price}$$
$$\text{Cap Rate} = 30,000 \div 500,000$$
$$= 0.06$$
$$= 6\%$$

This cap rate of 6% is then compared with the cap rates of other comparable properties in the market. An analysis finds that other comparable properties are selling with cap rates of 8%. We determine the sale price for this property at the market cap rate of 8%.

$$\text{Sale price} = \text{NOI} \div \text{cap rate}$$
$$= \$30,000 \div .08$$
$$= \$375,000$$

The sale price based on market conditions is $375,000, which is $125,000 less than the asking price. The asking price of $500,000 is not a fair price.

The cap rate is an important tool to use in assessing the value of income producing real estate of all sizes. However, the calculation is only as good as the choice of income producing properties used in establishing the market cap rate. Investors should evaluate as many income properties as they can to get the best idea of the market conditions and market prices to use in establishing a cap rate for comparison. Cap rates are also the basis for the income capitalization method of appraising property.

Net Income ROI

Net income ROI measures the relationship between net income and investment dollars. This measure is most useful for those who focus primarily on traditional income statements. Net income is income after all expenses are subtracted from gross revenues. These expenses are as reported in income statements. Net income is computed before and after taxes. When mortgage payments are considered, only the interest, tax, and insurance portion of the payment is included as an expense. The principal portion of the payment has no effect on an income statement. It is a balance sheet item, as opposed to an income statement item. When payment is paid to principal, cash reserves are reduced, and the loan balance is reduced. This creates a balance since an asset (cash) is used to reduce a liability (loan) by an equivalent amount. Net Income ROI is calculated as follows:

$$\text{Net Income ROI} = (\text{gross income} - \text{operating expenses} - \text{interest} - \text{depreciation}) \div \text{owner's equity}$$

Example:

An investor acquires a mortgage at 8% for 20 years with 2 points for an income property. The down payment was $300,000. The first year debt service was $50,186 and the principal was 10,568. The expenses of the property are as follows:

Property tax	$21,500
Insurance	$5,725
Repairs and maintenance	$10,500
Water	$8,250
Sewer	$2,000
Other miscellaneous expenses	$4,200
Total:	**$52,175.00**

The depreciation expense is $13,500, depreciable points are $500, and interest on the account of the property is $50. Gross income from the rents is $120,000 with a vacancy allowance of 2%. Net income ROI is calculated as:

Gross income	= income from rent – vacancy allowance	= $120,000 – $2,400	= $117,600
Operating expenses	= sum of all expenses		= $52,175
Interest	= debt service – principal	= $50,186 – $10,568	= $39,618
Depreciation	= real property + points	= $13,500 + $500	= $14,000

Net Income ROI = (gross income – operating expenses – interest – depreciation) ÷ owner's equity
= ($117,600 – $52,175 – $39,618 – $14,000) ÷ $300,000
= $11,807 ÷ $300,000
= 0.03695
= 3.70%

Cash ROI

Cash return on investment is also termed cash-on-cash return. Cash ROI measures the relationship between cash remaining after debt service and investment dollars. Cash ROI is also known as owner's equity. This ratio differs from net income ROI since it excludes all non-cash items, such as depreciation, and includes the non-income portion of the principal paid on loans. Investors tend to focus more on this measurement simply because it measures cash. Many investors prefer to analyze the relationship between their cash investments and the cash flow from those investments. The cash investment includes all the expenses required to acquire the investment property. Closing costs, loan fees, and monies spent for evaluation, such as feasibility studies, must be included for an accurate analysis. Cash ROI is calculated as follows:

Cash ROI = remaining cash after debt service ÷ cash investment

Example:

From the example above:

$$NOI = \text{gross income} + \text{interest} - \text{vacancy loss} - \text{expenses}$$
$$= \$120,000 + \$50 - \$2,400 - \$52,175$$
$$= \$65,475$$
$$\text{Cash ROI} = (NOI - \text{debt service}) \div \text{cash investment}$$
$$= 65,475 - 50,186 \div 300,000$$
$$= .0509$$
$$= 5.09\%$$

Total ROI

The total return on investment is similar to cash ROI except that total ROI includes the non-cash portion of return, namely a reduction in principal. This measure considers the portion of a loan that is reduced by payments made to the principal portion of a loan. Total ROI is the ratio of remaining cash after debt plus principle payments to cash investment dollars. Total ROI is calculated as follows:

Total ROI = (remaining cash after debt service + principal
reduction) ÷ cash investment

Example:

Continuing with the same example:

$$\text{Total ROI} = (\text{remaining cash after debt service} + \text{principal reduction}) \div \text{cash investment}$$
$$= 65{,}475 - 10{,}568 \div 300{,}000$$
$$= 0.18302$$
$$= 18.30\%$$

Debt Service Coverage Ratio (DSCR)

Debt service coverage ratio is a measure of the relationship between available cash after operating expenses have been paid to the cost required to make debt payments. When lenders lend money for investment properties, they want some assurance that the investment will generate enough income to service the debt. Lenders use this ratio to determine if a potential investment property generates enough cash to pay all debts and obligations of a property.

DSCR is calculated as follows:

$$\text{DSCR} = \frac{\text{NOI}}{\text{Principal} + \text{Interest}}$$

Lenders establish acceptable limits for the minimum DSCR, which may range from as low as 0.75% to as high as 1.4%, but often fall within the 1% to 1.2% range. A debt service ratio of 1% indicates that the property has income before debt service that is as much as the debt service. This means that the property generates net income equal to the amount needed to make mortgage payments. A DSCR of 1.2% indicates that the property generates 20% more net income than it needs to make mortgage payments. Several factors influence the value of DSCR. Longer amortization schedules, for example, reduce the monthly cash outflow from an investment property and leave more cash available to pay debts of the property. If an amortization period is increased, the monthly payment of the associated loan will decrease, which increases the value of the DSCR, since NOI is not affected by amortization.

Example:

An investor has mortgage payments of $28,000 on a rental unit with NOI of $32,000. The DSCR is calculated as:

$$DSCR = NOI \div (principal + interest)$$
$$= \$32,000 \div 28,000$$
$$= 1.14$$

The net income from the rental unit is 14% more than is needed for the mortgage payments.

Gross Rent Multiplier (GRM)

The gross rent multiplier is a measure of the relationship between an income property's total purchase price and the property's gross scheduled income. The GRM measures price to income and is similar to cap rate since it captures revenue and price. However, the GRM captures gross revenues, and the cap rate captures net revenues. The calculation for GRM is as follows:

$$GRM = purchase\ price \div gross\ scheduled\ income$$

The GRM and cap rate performance measures are inverted relative to one another. In the computation of GRM, price is the numerator, and in the computation of cap rate, price is the denominator. The lower the purchase price is relative to income and the higher the income is relative to price, the lower the ratios. A higher cap rate is preferred, and a lower GRM is preferred.

The calculation of GRM can be either on an as-is basis with no changes or improvements to the property or on a pro forma basis, which includes improvements and the expected increase in revenue from the improvements.

Example:

An investor paid $380,000 for a four-unit apartment house. Each apartment rents for $950 a month. It is estimated that good management could achieve a profit of 35% of gross income. The GRM is computed as follows:

$$\text{Annual rent} = \$950 * 4 * 12 = \$45,600$$
$$\text{Expected gross scheduled income} = 35\% * \$45,600 = \$15,960$$
$$\text{GRM} = \text{purchase price} \div \text{gross scheduled income}$$
$$= \$380,000 \div \$15,960$$
$$= 23.81$$

Operating Ratio (OR)

Operating ratio is a measure of the relationship between total operating expenses and gross operating income. The operating ratio provides a measure of how efficiently a property may be operated. The OR may range from as low as 30% to as high as 70% or more depending on the type of property. Commercial properties typically have a lower OR since most of the expenses of the property are paid by the tenant. Multifamily properties typically have higher measures of OR since the investor pays a larger portion of the expenses of the property, though this varies depending on established rental agreements. The operating ratio is calculated as follows:

$$\text{OR} = \text{total operating expenses} \div \text{gross operating income}$$

This measure requires that the investor properly account for all factors that contribute to operating expenses. A high OR may indicate that expenses are too high, while a low OR may indicate that expenses are not being reported or not properly recorded. If repairs are known to average 10 to 12% of gross operating income but are reported as 17%, either the repairs are too costly or the property is experiencing some difficulties. Likewise, if repairs are being reported as 5%, either the repairs are not being reported or the property is in exceptionally good condition.

Example:

The monthly rent from a rental unit is $1,200 with a vacancy allowance of 2%. The expenses of the property include:

Property tax	$1,500
Insurance	$725
Repairs and maintenance	$2,00
Other miscellaneous expenses	$4,200
Total:	$6,427.00

OR is calculated as follows:

$$\text{Gross income} = \$1,200 * 12 = \$14,400$$
$$\text{Gross operating income} = \$14,400 - (.02 * \$14,400)$$
$$= \$14,112$$

$$\text{OR} = \text{total operating expenses} \div \text{gross operating income}$$
$$= 6,427 \div 14,112$$
$$= 0.455$$

Breakeven Ratio (BER)

The breakeven ratio measures the relationship between total cash inflows and total cash outflows. The BER is similar to OR since the computation of both measures capture total operating expenses as part or all of the numerator and gross income as the denominator. The difference is that the BER captures debt service as part of the numerator. The BER provides a measure of cash flow from the property, and the OR provides a measure of income and expenses. The break-even point is the point at which total cash inflows are exactly equal to total cash outflows. A positive cash flow, which indicates that cash inflows exceed cash outflows, results in a BER that is less than 1. Conversely, a negative cash flow, which indicates that cash outflows exceed cash inflows, results in a BER that is greater than 1. At the break-even point the BER is equal to 1. The BER is calculated as follows:

$$BER = (total\ operating\ expense + debt\ service) \div gross\ operating\ income$$

Most lenders seek a BER of 85% or less. If the market indicates that occupancy rates are low, lenders may require a BER that is greater than the average occupancy rate. Low occupancy rates indicate that there is uncertainty in the potential income stream.

Example:

The mortgage payment on the example above is $800 per month. The BER is calculated as follows:

$$Debt\ service = \$800 * 12 = \$9,600$$
$$BER = (total\ operating\ expense + debt\ service) \div gross\ operating\ income$$
$$= (6,427 + 9,600) \div 14,112$$
$$= 1.1357$$

The BER is greater than 1, which indicates a negative cash flow.

Operating Efficiency Ratio (OER)

The operating efficiency ratio measures the operating expenses of an income property relative to the size of the property. This ratio measures dollars per square feet. Similar to the OR, the OER measures how efficiently a property can be operated. The OER measures efficiency relative to the square footage of a property; the OR measures efficiency relative to the income of the property.

Further, this performance measure may be used to compare similar properties. The calculation for OER is as follows:

$$\text{OER} = \text{total operating expenses} \div \text{square feet}$$

Example:

A lot that measures 600 x 600 feet is purchased as the site for a furniture store. The parking lot will consume 50% of the total area and is to be surfaced with rolled asphalt at a cost of $30 per square yard. Curbing is to be constructed around the entire perimeter of the lot at a cost of $20 per yard. The price for construction of the store is estimated to be $40 per square foot of floor space. An initial down payment of $678,000 was made to acquire the lot. The developers have established a capitalization rate of 10%, and the net profit is expected to be 30% of the gross income. The OR is computed as follows:

- The square footage of the lot is: 600 ft * 600 ft = 360,000 sq ft

- The parking lot measures 50% of the total area of the lot:
  .50 * 360,000 = 180,000 sq ft

- The cost of the asphalt for the parking lot is:

$$\frac{\$30}{\text{yard}} * \frac{\text{sq yard}}{9\text{ ft}^2} * 18,000 \text{ ft}^2 = \$600,000$$

- The footage of the curb is: 600 ft * 4 = 2,400 ft

- The cost of the curbing is:

$$2,400 \text{ ft} * \frac{\text{yard}}{3\text{ ft}} * \frac{\$20}{\text{yard}} = \$16,000$$

- The cost of the store is:

$$180{,}000 \text{ ft}^2 \; * \; \frac{\$40}{\text{ft}^2} \; = \; \$7{,}200{,}000$$

The total cost = cost of asphalt + cost of curbing + cost of store +
down payment
=$600,000 + $16,000 + $7,200,000 + $6,780,000
= $8,494,000

Income = total cost * cap rate
= $8,494,000 * .10
= $849,400

Profit is expected to be 30% of the gross income. So, expenses are expected to consume the other 70% of gross income.

Expenses = $849,400 * .70 = $594,580

OR = total operating expenses ÷ gross income
= $594,580 ÷ $849,400
= 0.07

OER = total operating expenses ÷ square feet
= $594,580 ÷ 180,000
= 3.3

CHAPTER 6

FINANCING MATHEMATICS

_____

INSTALLMENTS

Installment payments are often times misunderstood. There are many different types of installments and charges are not always calculated in the same manner. If the period of installment is more than one year, the rate may be based on the unpaid balance. This type of interest rate computation is similar to compound interest and will always be less than the corresponding simple interest rate.

Residuary Method

The residuary method is also called the merchant method of computing the rate charged on installment payments. This method assumes that each payment is used to repay the principal until the entire amount that is owed is paid. Subsequent payments are then used to pay the accumulated interest.

Example:

A loan of $500 is paid on installment with 12 equal monthly payments of $43.86. Since 12 * $43.86 = $526.32, the total charge for the loan is $526.32 – $500 = $26.32. Since the borrower is required to make monthly payments, the borrower only has full use of the base amount of $500 for one month. At the end of the first month, a payment of $43.86 is paid, such that the borrower now has use of $500 – $43.86 = $456.14 for one month. The the next payment is due one month later. At the end of the second month, the borrower makes another payment of $43.86, and the borrower now has use of $456.15 – $43.86 = $412.28 for 1 month. This process continues each month until the loan reaches its maturity of 12 months, as shown in the following schedule:

	Amount	Period
	$500.00	1st month
	$456.14	2nd month
	$412.28	3rd month
	$368.42	4th month
	$324.56	5th month
	$280.70	6th month
	$236.84	7th month
	$192.98	8th month
	$149.12	9th month
	$105.26	10th month
	$61.4	11th month
	$17.54	12th month
Total:	$3,105.24	12 months

The total outstanding balance for the year is $3,105.24. Though the borrower borrowed $500, the borrower actually had use of the equivalent of $3,105.24 for 1 month. Also, since the interest paid on the loan over the course of the year is equal to $26.32, that interest represents the cost to make use of $3,105.24 for $1/_{12}$ month.

This is the equivalent of $3,105.24 borrowed using simple interest at 10.17% since:

$$i = Prt$$
$$\$26.32 = \$3,105.24 * r * 1/12$$
$$r = \$26.32 * 12 \div \$3,105.24$$
$$= 0.1017$$
$$= 10.17\%$$

FHA Method

The FHA method is also called the constant-ratio method of computing installment rates. This method assumes that each payment is made up of two parts. The first part is the principal, and the second part is the interest. This method further assumes that the ratio of the two parts is equal.

From the example above, a loan of $500 is paid on installment with 12 equal monthly payments of $43.86. Since 12 * $43.86 = $526.32, the total charge for the loan is $26.32. If only the principal were to be paid with the 12 monthly payments, the amount of the payment would be $41.67 rather than $43.36. If only the interest amount of $26.32 were to be paid with the 12 monthly payments, the payment would be $2.19. As such, we can assume that the $43.86 payment is divided such that $41.67 of each payment is applied to principal, and $2.19 of each payment is considered interest.

The outstanding balance of which the borrower may make use of is shown in the following schedule.

	Amount	Period
	$500.00	1st month
	$458.33	2nd month
	$416.66	3rd month
	$374.99	4th month
	$333.32	5th month
	$291.65	6th month

	$249.98	7th month
	$208.31	8th month
	$166.64	9th month
	$124.97	10th month
	$83.30	11th month
	$41.63	12th month
Total:	$3,249.78	12 months

The total outstanding balance for the year is $3,249.78. The borrower actually had use of the equivalent of $3,249.78 for 1 month. This is the equivalent of $3,249.78 borrowed using simple interest at 9.71% since:

$$i = Prt$$
$$\$26.28 = \$3,249.78 * r * 1/12$$
$$r = \$26.28 * 12 \div \$3,249.78$$
$$= 0.097040415$$
$$= 9.71\%$$

VALUE OF NOTES

Discounts and Percentages

Discounts are most commonly used in retail markets to reward customers for their market share of purchases. Discounts are a reduction in price offered by wholesalers, manufacturers, and other vendors. Discount prices are less than the list prices established for an item or commodity. There are three primary types of discounts, namely trade discounts, series discounts, and cash discounts.

Trade Discounts

Any reduction from the list price is called a trade discount. A trade discount is a single discount that is usually stated as a percent of the list price. To find the amount of a trade discount, multiply the list price by the discount rate. As an example, a wholesaler lists doors at $140. The trade discount rate is 40%. The trade discount is calculated as follows:

$$\text{Discount} = \$140 * 40\% = \$140 * .40$$
$$= \$56$$

To find the net price of a door, deduct the trade discount from the list price as follows:

$$\text{Net Price} = \$140 - \$56$$
$$= \$84$$

Series Discounts

Series discounts may also be termed successive discounts or chain discounts. The net price of a series discount is the cost after all trade discounts have been applied. When more than one discount is applied to an item, each successive discount is computed on the resulting net price acquired after the preceding discount has been deducted. Successive discounts are not merely deducted from the list price.

As an example, a series of trade discount rates offered by a wholesaler are 15%, 10%, and 7(½)% on an item that costs $1,250. The series discount is calculated as follows:

		Discount			Net Price
1st discount	$1,250 * 15%	= $187.50	&	$1,250.00 – $187.50	= $1,062.50
2nd discount	$1,062.50 * 10%	= $106.25	&	$1,062.5 – $106.25	= $956.25
3rd discount	$956.25 * 7(1/2)%	= $71.72	&	$956.25 – $71.72	= $884.53
Total series discounts:		$365.47			

These calculations could be simplified if a single discount, equivalent to the series of discounts, is first determined. To find the single discount that is equivalent to a series of discounts, the "on" percentage must first be determined. An "on" percentage is the percentage which, when multiplied by the list price, gives the net price.

Calculating the Single Discount Equivalent of a Series Discount

Example 1

Let the cost of an item be considered as 100%. This is the list price percent. The series discounts from the previous example are 15%, 10%, and 7($\frac{1}{2}$)%. The single equivalent of the series discount and the "on" percentage may be calculated as follows:

List price per cent		100%
Deduct 15% of 100%	.15 * 1 = 15%	– 15%
		= 85%
Deduct 10% of 85%	.10 * .85 = 8.5%	– 8.5%
		= 76.5%
Deduct 7.5% of 76.5%	.075 * .765 = 5.7%	– 5.7%
		= 70.8%

The "on" percentage, also known as the net price per cent, is 70.8%

$$\text{The single discount equivalent}$$
$$= \text{list price per cent} - \text{the net price per cent}$$
$$= 100\% - 70.8\%$$
$$= 29.2\%$$

The single discount of 29.2% is the equivalent of the series discounts, 15%, 10%, and 7($\frac{1}{2}$)%.

The total series discount

$$= 29.2\% \text{ of } \$1{,}250$$
$$= .292 * \$1{,}250$$
$$= \$365$$

(as calculated in the previous example)

Example 2

An alternate method involves subtracting each discount per cent from 100% and finding the product of the remainders. The single discount per cent equivalent is then calculated as the difference between the final product and 100%. This alternative method for the previous problem is as follows:

$$100\% - 15\% = 85\%$$
$$100\% - 10\% = 90\%$$
$$100\% - 7(1/2)\% = 92.5\%$$

$$85\% * 90\% * 92.5\%$$
$$= .85 * .90 * .925$$
$$= 0.71$$
$$= 71\%$$

(this is the same as that calculated above)

Example 3

Another method that may be used when the series discount includes only two discounts involves subtracting the product of the discounts from the sum of the two discounts. The following example uses this shorter method to find the single discount equivalent of the two discounts, 20% and 15%.

The sum of the two discount percent is calculated as:
$$20\% + 15\% = 35\%$$

The product of the two discount percent is calculated as:
$$20\% * 15\% = 3\%$$

The difference between the sum and the product is:
$$35\% - 3\% = 32\%$$

Therefore, a single discount of 32% is equivalent to two discounts of 20% and 15%.

Cash Discounts

Cash discounts are offered for the prompt payment of accounts. If payment is made immediately or within a specified amount of time, a cash discount is offered at a predetermined rate. The terms of the discount are often specified in a format similar to: Terms: 2/10n/30. The first value specifies the discount rate—in this instance, 2%. The second value specifies the number of days, from the date of purchase or the date of invoice, for which for the discount will be applicable—in this instance, 10 days net. The final value specifies the time, from the date of purchase or date of invoice, that is allowed to expire before the balance is due in full. Other notations that may be used include E O M and Extra. E O M means "end of month," but it may be interpreted differently in other industries or with other companies. E O M indicates that the time for allowing discounts is measured from the end of the month rather than the date of purchase or date of invoice. If the terms of discount on an invoice dated July 10 are specified as Terms: 2/10 E O M, the purchaser may deduct a 2% discount if payment is made before October 10. If the invoice is dated after the 25th day of the month, the terms often refer to the following month. If an invoice is dated July 27 with terms specified as Terms 2/10 EOM, the discount applies until September 10. The notation, Extra, indicates that the discount may be applied for the specified number of days in addition to any previously indicated terms. If the terms of an invoice are specified as 2/10 60 Extra, the purchaser may take a cash discount of 2% for the first 10 days plus an additional 60 days. The invoice specifies a total of 70 days to take the discount.

Percentage Increase

Many problems arise in which the amount is known, and it is necessary to find the base. When a percentage is added to a given base, the resulting sum is called the amount. If 12% was added to $1,000, the increase would be $120 and the total amount = $1,000 + $120 = $1,120. As such, the amount is 12% greater than the base or 112% of the base. If it is known that an amount is $1,120 and this amount represents 12% more than the base, the base can be found by dividing the amount by the sum of 100% and the percent increase.

$$Base = \$1,120 \div 112\%$$
$$= \$1,120 \div 1.12$$
$$= \$1,000$$

Percentage Decrease

Problems will also arise in which it is necessary to find a percentage decrease. A difference is the amount obtained when a percentage is deducted from the base. The base is equal to the sum of the difference and percentage. Often, the base is known, and it necessary to find the difference and percentage.

Example:

A partial payment of $847.70 is made on a $1,000 invoice during the discount period. The discount is 2%. Payment of the total invoice during the discount period would be:

$$\$1,000 - 2\% * \$1000$$
$$= \$1000 - \$200$$
$$= \$980$$

This payment is 2% less than the invoiced amount, and the discount implies that, for each $0.98 paid during the discount period, $1 would be applied to the account since, by proportion, ($980 ÷ $1,000) = ($0.98 ÷ $1.00).

As such, the partial payment of $847.70 should be applied at the same rate.

$$\frac{\$980}{\$1,000} = \frac{\$847.70}{x}$$

Solve for x:

$$x = \frac{847.70 * 1,000}{980}$$

$$x = \$865$$

So, the partial payment of $847.70 made during the discount period will be applied to the debt as $865.

ANNUITIES

Annuities are a series of equal payments made at regular intervals for a predetermined period of time. Time intervals may be monthly, quarterly, semi-annually, or annually. Payments made on insurance policies and installment plans are examples of annuities. The term of the annuity is the length of time for which payments are made. The time between payments is the payment interval. If the term of an annuity is definite, such as 9 months or 5 years, the annuity is called an annuity certain. The terms of an annuity may not always be certain, such as with life insurance. The annuity is paid only during the life of the insured. In the case of uncertainty, the annuity is called a contingent annuity.

To calculate the payment for an annuity, certain factors must be defined:

n = the number of periods
R = periodic rent or the amount of each payment

i = rate of interest per period

S_n = the amount of an annuity; the sum of the accumulated payments at a given period in time (also called the accumulated amount of an annuity)

Term = the length of time for which payments are to continue as measured from the beginning of the first period to the end of the last period

Interval = interval between payments

An annuity is a form of geometric progression. S_n represents the sum of the series of values in the progression, while n represents the number of terms in the progression.

$$S_n = R * \frac{(1 + i)^n - 1}{i}$$

With the use of an annuity table, the value of 1 per period for an annuity of n = number of periods at i = interest rate may be found and:

$$S_n = R * s_{n|i}$$

Present Value

With annuities, it is more important to be able to determine the present value of a series of future payments rather than find the amount of such payments. The present value of an annuity and the amount of an annuity represent the same thing but from different points in time.

The present value of an annuity is represented by $A_{n'}$ = the sum of the present value for each of the future payments. The present value, if invested now, at rate i per period, would provide income sufficient to make future payments on the annuity. By definition:

$$A_n (1 + i)^n = R * \frac{(1 + i)^n - 1}{i}$$

$$A_n = R * \frac{1 - (1 + i)^{-n}}{i}$$

Further, the present value of an annuity of 1 per period is:

$$A_n = \frac{1 - (1 + i)^{-n}}{i}$$

The notation $a_{n|i}$ is used to represent the present value of an annuity of 1, at rate (i), is used in the calculation of present value as follows:

$$A_n = R * a_{n|t}$$

This formula relies on the value of $a_{n|t}$ as determined from the values in an annuity table. The value of a particular rate and period can be retrieved from the table. If the table does not provide a sought rate and period, a more complete annuity table may be sought from a number of print or online references. However, if a more complete table is not available, values of annuities for periods beyond the table may be found by separating the annuity into two separate annuities whose values are available in the table and considering each annuity separately. The value of the first annuity is taken from the table. The present worth of the second annuity at the beginning of its life is also taken from the table. The present worth of the second annuity is found by multiplying its tabular value by the tabular value for the first annuity.

Time Determination

It sometimes may be necessary to determine the length of time required for an annuity to accumulate to a certain amount or determine how many payments are necessary to discharge a debt.

Such times may be determined by the formula:

$$s_{n|i} = S_n \div R$$

When the number of payments results in a fractional value, the first n-1 payments accumulate to the whole portion of the fractional amount, while the fractional portion of the payment amount may be applied by one of two methods:

(1) Increase the amount of the last full payment. This is the most prevalent practice.

(2) Reduce the amount of the last payment to an amount that is smaller than all other payment amounts.

Example:

An investor needs to accumulate $3,200 for an investment. The investor puts $50 in a savings account at the end of the month. Money is worth 3% compounded monthly. We want to determine how many deposits are required to reach the $3,200 amount.

R = $50
$i = 3\% \div 12 = {}^1/_4\%$
S_n = $3,200

$$s_{n|i} = S_n \div R$$
$$= 3200 \div 50$$
$$= \$64$$

For ${}^1/_4\%, S_n$ = $64.65 in 60 intervals. So, 60 deposits of $1 will accumulate to $64.65. It follows that 60 deposits of $50 will accumulate to $50 * 64.65 = $3,232.34. The amount repaid in 60 intervals is more than the target amount of $3,200. So, the last payment (60th) will be a partial payment. To compute the partial payment amount, subtract the target amount from the amount accumulated in 60 intervals. The result is the discount on the $50 payment.

$$\$3{,}232.34 - \$3{,}200 = \$32.34$$
$$\text{So, the last payment is } \$50 - \$32.34 = \$17.66$$

Amortization

When a debt is to be repaid in equal installments of principal and interest, the payment is amortized. The payment necessary to discharge the debt is an annuity with present value equal to the original principal of the debt. As such, the total of the payments made under amortization will be greater than the original amount of the debt.

Amortized loans offer the benefit of having payments spread out over the life of the loan, and the borrower may easily assess his or her position with the loan. All home loans guaranteed by the FHA, and most other property loans, are financed by amortized mortgages.

Although payments on amortized loans are equal, the division of principal and interest varies from period to period. An amortization schedule is usually prepared to show how payments are apportioned. In the absence of an amortization schedule, the amount of unpaid principle may be calculated at any given time using one of the following two methods:

- **Prospective method.** Calculate the remaining principal as the present value of the future remaining payments.

- **Retrospective method.** The outstanding debt is equal to the original debt plus all accumulated interest to date minus the amount of all the payments that have been made. This method may be used if the number of total payments is unknown or if the last payment is not the same as all other payments.

The periodic payment of an annuity is called the rent of an annuity and is represented by the symbol R. To find the periodic rent when the amount or present value of the annuity is known:

$$A_n = R\, a_{n|i}$$

Then, by definition, the rate is calculated as follows:

$$R = A_n\, (1 \div a_{n|i})$$

Example:

A debt of $42,000 bearing interest at 4% is to be amortized by payments in 6-month intervals for the next five years. The periodic payment is computed as follows:

$$A_n = \$42,000$$
$$i = 4\% \div 2 = 2\%$$
$$n = 2 * 5 = 10$$

The value of the note at maturity is calculated as $S = P\,(1 + i)^n$; where:

$$R = A_n\,(1 \div a_{n|i})$$
$$R = A_5\,(1 \div a_{5|2\%})$$
$$= \$42,000 * (1 \div 8.98258501)$$
$$= \$42,000 * .111326527$$
$$= \$467.57$$

The amortization schedule is as follows:

Period	Outstanding Principal Beginning of the Period	Interest 2%	Payment	Principal Repaid
1	$4,200	$84.00	$467.57	$383.57
2	$3,816.43	$76.33	$467.57	$391.24
3	$3,425.19	$68.50	$467.57	$399.07
4	$3,026.12	$60.52	$467.57	$407.05

5	$2,619.07	$52.38	$467.57	$415.19
6	$2,230.88	$44.08	$467.57	$423.29
7	$1,708.39	$35.61	$467.57	$431.96
8	$1,348.43	$26.97	$467.57	$440.60
9	$907.83	$18.16	$467.57	$449.41
10	$458.42	$9.17	$467.57	$458.40

Sinking Fund Amortization

When a debt is not amortized, the borrower must make provisions to pay the debt at maturity. Even when payment to the lender is not due until maturity, a contractual agreement may specify that payments be periodically deposited into a fund. That fund should equal the debt amount at maturity. Any fund established for such a purpose is called a sinking fund. A sinking fund is held for the purpose of meeting an obligation that is due in the future. Payments to a sinking fund are not required to be equal. Payments are often times determined as a percentage of earnings and may vary from period to period as earnings fluctuate. When equal payments are made to a sinking fund, periodically, the payments form an annuity. Determining the amount of each payment involves finding the rent of an annuity when the amount of the annuity is known. The value of $s_{n|i}$ can be found in an annuity table.

$$R = S_n (1 \div s_{n|i})$$

With an ordinary annuity, the present value is determined one payment interval before the first payment. A deferred annuity is a series of payments where the valuation date of the series of payments precedes the first payment date by more than one payment interval. The present value of a deferred annuity is equal to the present value of the annuity at the beginning of the annuity, discounted to the valuation date.

Example:

A company has a debt of $1,000,000 that is due in 10 years. The debt is to be discharged by a sinking fund, and the debtor is required to make semiannual contributions to the fund. Interest paid on the fund is 3%, converted semiannually. The total periodic charge for the debt is computed as follows:

$$S_n = \$1,000,000$$
$$i = 3\% \div 2 = 1(1/2)\%$$
$$n = 2 * 10 = 20$$
$$R = S_n \ (1 \div s_{n|i})$$
$$R = \$1,000,000 \ (1 \div s_{20|1(1/2)\%})$$
$$= \$1,000,000 \ * \ (.043245736)$$
$$= \$43,245.74$$

If the debt were interest bearing, bearing interest at 6%, the periodic contribution would remain the same. However, interest must be paid semiannually at 3% on the $1,000,000. That adds an additional .03 * $1,000,000 = $30,000 to the periodic payment. The total periodic payment is then $30,000 + $43,245.74 = $73,245.74.

BONDS

Small amounts of money can usually be borrowed from one lender, but large amounts of money are usually borrowed from many lenders. Many successful investors believe there is less risk involved if their investments are spread among several entities rather than being concentrated with any one entity. When a corporation, government entity, or business needs to borrow large amounts of money for a long period of time, they often seek funds from different lenders. To facilitate such lending, the borrower issues certificates, known as bonds, which indicate the terms for which the borrower borrows the money. Bonds may differ in type, but most bonds conform to a well-defined pattern. This discussion is limited to the most common type of bond, the standard bond pattern. Savings bonds, or Series E Bonds, which are issued by the federal government, are a special type of bond that has no similarity to typical corporate bonds, which are being discussed here. Other bonds issued by the federal government tend to follow the more conventional patterns.

One of the common characteristics of standard bond patterns is that each bond certificate specifies a date, called the date of maturity. The date of maturity is the date on which a corporation will pay the bondholder a designated amount of money, which is known as the redemption value of the bond. Usually, the redemption value paid on the maturity date is equal to the par, also known as the face value. The face value is the amount stated on a bond. Par is generally $1,000 or multiples of $1,000 since most investors find $1,000 to be a desirable minimum with which to deal. Occasionally bonds with a face value of $100 or $500 are issued, but they cause unnecessary work for the issuer, and they carry no offsetting advantages.

Coupon Rate

Another common characteristic of standard types of bonds is that the certificates indicate the rate of interest to be paid and the frequency with which payments are to be paid. The rate of interest is usually called the coupon rate. Interest is paid semiannually on the date specified in the bond. The number of payments made annually is standard, but the total number of payments varies. The coupon rate should not change or be modified during the period of a bond. Though every bond has an associated coupon rate, the rate is not uniform among bonds. Bond rates are usually referred to as x% bonds where x represents the rate that is stated. However, a semiannual bond interest payment equals only one-half of the stated coupon rate.

Many bonds include coupons, which are drawn in an amount equal to the semiannual interest payment. Such bonds are called coupon bonds. Each coupon is dated with the particular day on which the interest payment is due. The bondholder need only detach the coupon on the specified date and deposit it in the bank in the same manner that a check is deposited in the bank. As such, a bond coupon is much like a postdated check that cannot be cashed until the specified date. It is the responsibility of the bondholder to know when to cash the bond and collect the interest.

Many bonds are issued such that the owner may register the bond in his or her name with the issuing corporation. The corporation is then responsible for issuing the registered owner a check for the interest payment on the payment date. If the bond is sold, the new owner registers the bond in his or her name to receive the interest payments.

Many leading newspapers advertise the daily price quotations for bonds. Books, known a bond guides, are published monthly and made available at all brokerage houses and most banks and public libraries. Usually a single line is devoted to a single bond. A bond issued by Eastern Gas Company may be listed as "Eastern Gas Company 3's '07 Ms." The "3's" in the entry indicates that the interest rate is 3%, paid semiannually. The "'07" indicates that the maturity date is in 2007. The "Ms" indicates that interest is to be paid semiannually in March and September. The capital "M" signifies that the bond was issued in March rather than September, which is represented by lowercase "s." The maturity date is March 2007.

Yield Rate

When bonds are established as marketable bonds, it is expected that they will be freely bought and sold among investors. Marketable bonds differ from certain types of government issued bonds that are nontransferable, such as savings bonds. Under a standard bond contract, after a corporation has sold a bond, the corporation has no responsibility to return the principal until the date of maturity. As such, an original purchaser must wait for maturity to redeem a bond and receive the principal that was made for the bond. If, however, the purchaser wants the money before maturity, the purchaser may sell the bond to another investor.

Bonds, like anything else that is bought and sold, are expected to be subjected to some degree of price fluctuation. A bond bought at a price that is equal to the face value of the bond is bought par. A bond bought for less than the face value of the bond is bought at a discount. A bond bought for more than the face value of the bond is bought at premium. The rate of return received by an investor is known as the yield or yield rate. When a bond is bought at par, the rate of return is equal to the coupon rate. When a bond is bought at a price above the redemption price, the yield is less than the coupon rate.

If a 6% bond is bought for $1,000 with a one-year maturity, the purchaser can expect to receive $60 in interest plus the principal at maturity. If changes affect the bond market such that new bonds are being issued with 3% yield, an investor has the choice of purchasing new bonds with 3% yield or purchasing bonds that had been issued in the past at 6% yield. The investor must consider the return on investment for both options.

Example:

An investor has an offer to buy a $1,000 bond with 6% yield at premium for an amount equal to $1,020 or to buy newly issued bonds at par with 3% interest. An initial investment in the bond bought at par is $1,000, while the initial investment in the bond bought at premium would be $1,020. At maturity, the investor would receive $1,060 on the bond bought at premium. That is the face value of the bond plus interest at 6%, which is $60. Since the initial investment amount was $1,020, the income to the investor at maturity would be $,1060 – $1,020 = $40. Since the return on the initial $1,020 investment is $40 ÷ $1,020 = 3.92%, the investor receives more on the bond purchased at premium than he would receive for the purchase of a newly issued bond at par, since 3.92% is more than 3%.

	Premium	Par
Face Value	$1,000	$1,000
Interest	6%	3%
Initial Investment	$1,020	$1,000
Redemption Amount	$1,060	$1,030
Return	$40	$30
Yield	3.92%	3%

Conversely, if new bonds are being sold with 6% yield, an investor who holds bonds with 3% yield should not expect to sell his or her bonds at par value. The purchaser would expect to be able to purchase such bonds at a considerable discount to receive a return equivalent to or in excess of that offered for the newly issued bonds. The 3% bonds must be sold at a discount of at least $970 in order to receive an equivalent return. This represents a yield of $60 ÷ $970 = 6.19%.

	Discount	Par
Face Value	$1,000	$1,000
Interest	3%	6%
Initial Investment	$970	$1,000
Redemption Amount	$1,030	$1,060
Return	$60	$60
Yield	6.19%	6%

In the mathematics of finance, two principal types of problems occur involving bonds. They include determining the yield received on bonds bought at premium or discount and determining the price to pay for bonds to obtain a desirable yield.

The value of a bond is equal to the present value of the redemption price and the present value of an annuity of future payments, both evaluated at the desired rate of yield.

Let:

F = the face value of the bond

V = the value of the bond at the desired yield to maturity

r = the coupon rate per period

R = the amount of each periodic interest payment; if the bond is a coupon bond, then $R = F*r$

i = the yield rate per period on the present value

n = the number of interest periods to maturity; if the bond is a coupon bond, then n is the number of coupons still attached to the bond.

The present value of the principal is calculated as follows:

$$PV = F(1 + i)^{-n}$$

The present values of the income (R) is calculated as:

$$R * a_{n|i}$$

The sum of these two present values represents the present value of a bond to achieve the desired yield as follows:

$$V = F(1 + i)^{-n} + R * a_{n|i}$$

The value of the bond (V) may differ from the price of a bond since bond prices are quoted as a percentage of the face amount. A minimum variation in the price of $1/_8$% is the equivalent of \$1.25 on a $1,000 bond. As such, any bond whose value falls within the range of $950.625 and $951.875 is priced at $95(^1/_8)$.

Callable Bonds

When a corporation issues a bond, the corporation usually includes a provision that allows the corporation to pay the bond before maturity if the corporation chooses to do so. Such prepayment is an option, and as such, the purchaser does not have to agree to have the principal returned early unless there is some form of compensation to the purchaser for having to find another outlet for the investment dollars being returned. Such compensation is usually paid on the basis of established call prices. Call prices are a series of redemption amounts that are paid when a bond is called early. The redemption amount is a premium paid above par. As an example, a 10-year bond may be callable at 104% of its face value. Since, at maturity, 100% would be paid, the call prices may be established such that the bond is callable at the following series of dates:

Call Price	Redemption Period
104%	At 1 year
103%	At 3 years
102%	At 5 years
101%	Until maturity
100%	At maturity

Government bonds may be issued with two dates: one date signifying the date of bond maturity and the other date signifying the earliest year in which the bond may be called. In most instances such bonds may be called at par at any time after the first call date. Since a bond called at premium before maturity increases the yield, the yield is often computed to the maturity date. When a bond is called at par before maturity, the lower of two yields is determined: the yield to the earliest call date and the yield to maturity. The conservative approach is to assume the lowest yield. If a bond is bought at premium and called at par before maturity, the yield is computed to the nearest call date. If the bond is paid at par on that date, the premium would have to be written off more rapidly than if the bond is not paid until maturity. If the bond is bought at discount and called at par before maturity, the yield is computed to the maturity date. Calling the bond at an earlier date results in a higher, rather than a lower, yield.

An investor may not know that a corporate bond is going to be called at a premium until the corporation issues such an announcement. Further, the investor will not know the contractual provisions under which the corporation will call the bond. As such, the yield on corporate bonds is determined based on the redemption value, which is equal to the par value. If the price of the bond is at or near the call price, the investor may hesitate to take a position, which will lower or negate the yield if the bond is called in the near future. The investor would need to compute potential yields under varying assumptions to arrive at an investment decision. A bond is valued and the yield is computed on assumptions, which provides the lower yield. If corporate bonds are called after they have been acquired, the yield may turn out to be materially different from the anticipated yield.

Perpetuities

Some government and corporate bonds are issued without a maturity date. The interest payments are expected to continue forever. Such bonds are considered to be continuing in perpetuity, which is any series of payments that are to continue for an unlimited period of time. The amount of interest on a perpetual bond does not change.

The value of a bond as a perpetuity is determined by the minimum rate of income that an investor is willing to accept.

Example:

The rate on a bond with a par value of $1,000 is 4%. If an investor is willing to accept a 5% return on the bond, the value of the bond is as follows:

Let:
x = the value of the bond = $1,000
i = yield = 5%
R = periodic payment = $40
yield * value = periodic income

$$PV \text{ (perpetuity)} = R \div i$$
$$value = periodic\ income \div yield$$
$$= \$40 \ / \ 5\%$$
$$= \$800$$

A perpetuity having payments of R is considered a capitalized value of R.

A prime example of perpetuity is the money donated to colleges and universities. The income from such funds, for example, is expected to permanently provide enough money to pay the salary of a professor of a particular subject. The donator is said to endow a chair in the subject matter. Other examples are the establishment of a fund for the perpetual care of a cemetery or a preferred stock on which dividends are paid that has no maturity date. Investors will attempt to appraise perpetuity.

Capitalized Cost of Bonds

When a factory is built, a library established, or a house is painted, provisions may be made for the periodic replacement or maintenance. A fund may be created to provide for such periodic demands on a periodic basis. A similar situation is created when it is necessary to compare or contrast the total future expense of a method, plan, machine, or part. A fund S must be established with periodic demand k.

The capitalized cost K is defined as the original cost plus the present value of an unlimited number of future renewals of an asset. The fund must be sufficiently large to meet the original cost C and to provide S dollars every k periods. The PV of periodic income of R dollars is $R \div i$. When payment is not needed every period but only every k periods, the value of the annuity is $S \div i$ at the end of k periods. As such, the present value of amounts needed for periodic replacement every k periods or the capitalized cost of K is:

$$K = C + \frac{S}{i} * \frac{1}{s_{k|i}}$$

If assets must be replaced in their entirety every k periods, then C = S, and the formula for the capitalized cost of k becomes:

$$K = \frac{S}{i} * \frac{1}{a_{k|i}}$$

Example:

In determining the cost of a roof for a garage, an investor needs to determine whether a shingle roof that cost $600 and is expected to last for 8 years is cheaper or more costly than a composite roof that cost $400 and is expected to last for 5 years. Money is worth 5%.

The capitalized cost of the shingle roof is:
S = $600
k = 8
i = 5%

$$K = (S \div I) * (1 \div a_{k|i})$$
$$= (\$600 \div 5\%) * (1 \div a_{8|5\%})$$
$$= (\$600 \div .05) * (1 \div 6.46321276)$$
$$= \$12,000 * 0.154721813$$
$$= \$1,856.661756$$
$$= \$1,856.66$$

The capitalized cost of the composite roof is:

S = \$400

k = 5

i = 5%

$$K = (S \div I) * (1 \div a_{k|i})$$
$$= (\$400 \div 5\%) * (1 \div a_{5|5\%})$$
$$= (\$400 \div .05) * (1 \div 4.32947667)$$
$$= \$8,000 * 0.230974798$$
$$= \$1,847.798385$$
$$= \$1,847.80$$

The capitalized cost of the composite roof is $1,856.66 – $1,847.80 = $8.86 cheaper than the capitalized cost of the shingle roof.

EXCEL FUNCTIONS

Many of the computations presented in this book may be performed using the Microsoft® Excel spreadsheet or some other familiar spreadsheet package. A spreadsheet may eliminate the sometimes time consuming task of performing computations by hand. Excel provides an array of built in functions that will assist the user in building a formula. A function is a predefined equation that operates on one or more variables and returns a single value. Excel includes several hundred functions in different categories.

Excel processes functions that are expressed with a specific syntax or structure. The syntax includes abbreviated words that serve as the function name and arguments to the function. For example, the syntax for the function that returns the number of periods for an investment is NPER. The syntax of the NPER function is as follows:

NPER(rate,pmt,pv,fv,type)

The inputs to the function are the variables enclosed in parentheses. These variables are called arguments of the function. The arguments are rate, payment amount, present value, future value, and type. A value must be specified for each argument, and a comma must separate those arguments. When an argument is zero, the zero need not be specified, but the comma must still be included. If the pmt argument, for example, is equal to zero, the syntax of the function would be as follows:

$$NPER(rate,,pv,fv,type)$$

Note that two commas are included in succession to represent the null argument. More advanced Excel users may input functions directly from the keyboard, but Excel provides a built in tool to build such functions.

To access Excel's built in functions, choose "Functions" on the Insert menu pull-down box and a new widow will appear as shown in Figure 6. The left pane of the window will show the categories of functions available, and the right windowpane will show all available functions under a specific category of functions. Choosing the "Financial" category of functions on the left pane provides access to the functions listed in the table below:

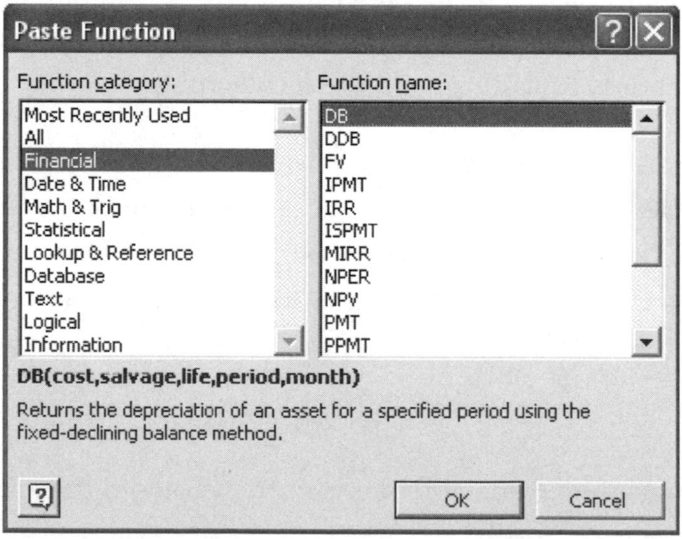

Figure 6: Excel Insert Functions Window

Once a particular function is chosen, a new window appears that allows the user to input variables to satisfy the function, as shown at Figure 6. The "tab" key is used to move from one input variable to another. Note that values are input without the use of dollar signs and commas. To assist users in inputting the proper values, Excel provides an explanation of each of the input variables in the lower pane of the window. The cursor must be in an input box before the explanation for that variable appears. In addition, the result of the function is visible in the lower pane so that the user may see the answer and make modifications, if necessary, before actually adding the result to the worksheet page. Users must click the "OK" button to have the result placed on the worksheet page. The result will be placed on the worksheet in the cell the cursor was occupying before inserting the function.

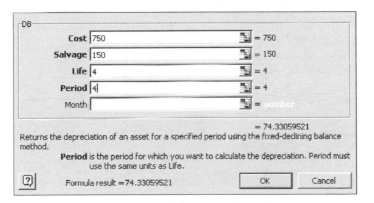

Figure 7: Excel DB Function Window

The DB function computation shown in Figure 7 indicates that an asset that cost $750 with a salvage value of $150 and a life of 4 years has a depreciation amount of $74.33 at the end of 4 years. No value is input for the Month variable since the default value is 12. The more experienced Excel user would be capable of inputting the formula directly into the worksheet cell. The formula created from Excel's built in formula generator is:

$$=DB(750,150,4,4)$$

Example:

We will use the FV function to find the future value of an investment. The amount of $2,200 is compounded for 8 years at 5(1/2)%, converted semiannually, and entered into the formula at Figure 8. The input variables are rate, number of payments, payment amount, present value, and type. Not all the input values need to be defined to solve this particular problem. We have not established a payment amount. Note that Excel requires present value to be expressed as a negative number. From an investment perspective, PV represents outgoing money while FV represents incoming money. The future value of $2,250 is calculated as $3453.04. The equivalent formula is:

$$=FV(0.055,8,,-2250)$$

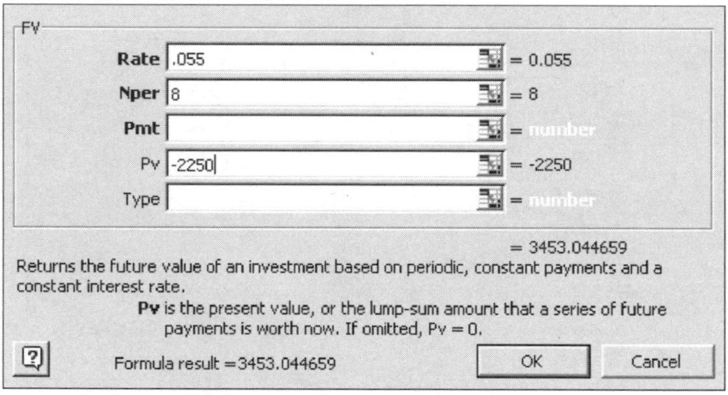

Figure 8: Excel FV Function Window

The input may be a single value or range of data. In Excel, data is arranged in columns or rows on a worksheet. These columns and rows of data may serve as the input range for computations. Columns and rows of data may be given names, called range names, which are used as arguments in Excel functions.

There are two ways to create a name range. The first is to select the range of cells to be named. Click the Name box, type in an unused range name, and press enter. Range names must begin with a letter and cannot include spaces.

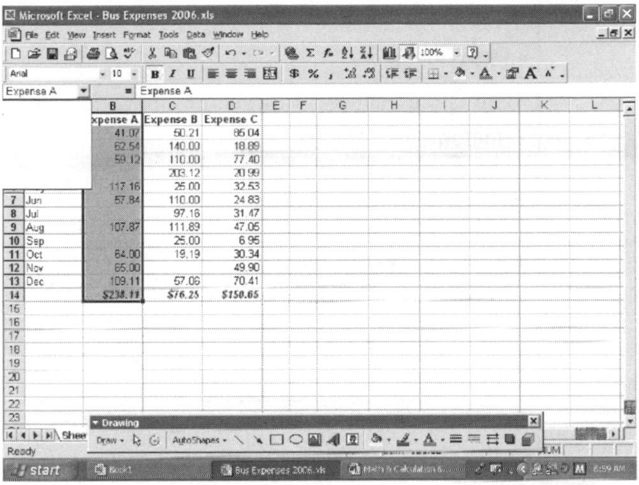

Figure 9: Create a Range Name Using the Name Box

The other way to create a range name is to use the Create command from the Insert pull down menu on the toolbar.

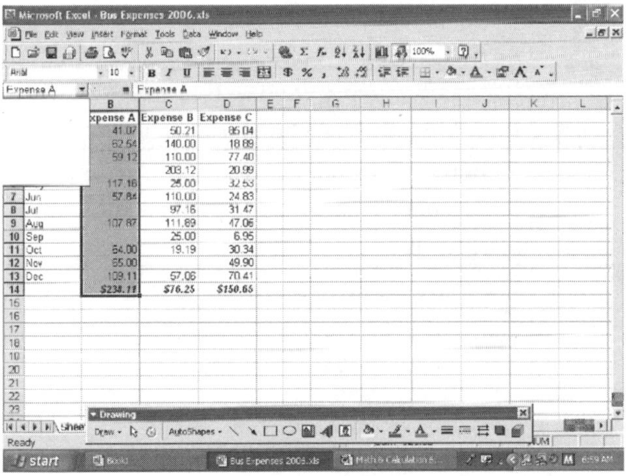

Figure 10: Create a Range Name Using the Insert Command

Microsoft® Excel provides the following financial functions. However, a number of Excel templates can be found online that provide functions specific to real estate analysis and other disciplines.

ACCRINT	Returns the accrued interest for a security that pays periodic interest
ACCRINTM	Returns the accrued interest for a security that pays interest at maturity
AMORDEGRC	Returns the depreciation for each accounting period
AMORLINC	Returns the depreciation for each accounting period
COUPDAYBS	Returns the number of days from the beginning of the coupon period to the settlement date
COUPDAYS	Returns the number of days in the coupon period that contains the settlement date
COUPDAYSNC	Returns the number of days from the settlement date to the next coupon date
COUPNCD	Returns the next coupon date after the settlement date
COUPNUM	Returns the number of coupons payable between the settlement date and maturity date
COUPPCD	Returns the previous coupon date before the settlement date
CUMIPMT	Returns the cumulative interest paid between two periods
CUMPRINC	Returns the cumulative principal paid on a loan between two periods
DB	Returns the depreciation of an asset for a specified period using the fixed-declining balance method
DDB	Returns the depreciation of an asset for a specified period using the double-declining balance method or some other method you specify
DISC	Returns the discount rate for a security
DOLLARDE	Converts a dollar price, expressed as a fraction, into a dollar price, expressed as a decimal number
DOLLARFR	Converts a dollar price, expressed as a decimal number, into a dollar price, expressed as a fraction
DURATION	Returns the annual duration of a security with periodic interest payments
EFFECT	Returns the effective annual interest rate
FV	Returns the future value of an investment
FVSCHEDULE	Returns the future value of an initial principal after applying a series of compound interest rates
INTRATE	Returns the interest rate for a fully invested security

IPMT	Returns the interest rate for a fully invested security
IRR	Returns the internal rate of return for a series of cash flows
ISPMT	Calculates the interest paid during a specific period of an investment
MDURATION	Returns the Macauley modified duration for a security with an assumed par value of $100
MIRR	Returns the internal rate of return where positive and negative cash flows are financed at different rates
NOMINAL	Returns the annual nominal interest rate
NPER	Returns the number of periods for an investment
NPV	Returns the net present value of an investment based on a series of periodic cash flows and a discount rate
ODDFPRICE	Returns the price per $100 face value of a security with an odd first period
ODDFYIELD	Returns the yield of a security with an odd first period
ODDLPRICE	Returns the price per $100 face value of a security with an odd last period
ODDLYIELD	Returns the yield of a security with an odd last period
PMT	Returns the periodic payment for an annuity
PPMT	Returns the payment on the principal for an investment for a given period
PRICE	Returns the price per $100 face value of a security that pays periodic interest
PRICEDISC	Returns the price per $100 face value of a discounted security
PRICEMAT	Returns the price per $100 face value of a security that pays interest at maturity
PV	Returns the present value of an investment
RATE	Returns the interest rate per period of an annuity
RECEIVED	Returns the amount received at maturity for a fully invested security
SLN	Returns the straight-line depreciation of an asset for one period
SYD	Returns the sum of years' digits depreciation of an asset for a specified period
TBILLEQ	Returns the bond-equivalent yield for a Treasury bill

TBILLPRICE	Returns the price per $100 face value for a Treasury bill
TBILLYIELD	Returns the yield for a Treasury bill
VDB	Returns the depreciation of an asset for a specified or partial period using a declining balance method
XIRR	Returns the internal rate of return for a schedule of cash flows that is not necessarily periodic
XNPV	Returns the net present value for a schedule of cash flows that is not necessarily periodic
YIELD	Returns the yield on a security that pays periodic interest
YIELDDISC	Returns the annual yield for a discounted security; for example, a Treasury bill
YIELDMAT	Returns the annual yield of a security that pays interest at maturity

APPENDICES

APPENDIX 1: CHART OF NUMBERED DAYS FOR A CALENDAR YEAR

Number for Each Day of the Year											
Day	Jan	Feb	Mar	Apr	May	Jun	Jul	Aug	Sep	Oct	Nov	Dec
1	1	32	60	91	121	152	182	213	244	274	305	335
2	2	33	61	92	122	153	183	214	245	275	306	336
3	3	34	62	93	123	154	184	215	246	276	307	337
4	4	35	63	94	124	155	185	216	247	277	308	338
5	5	36	64	95	125	156	186	217	248	278	309	339
6	6	37	65	96	126	157	187	218	249	279	310	340
7	7	38	66	97	127	158	188	219	250	280	311	341
8	8	39	67	98	128	159	189	220	251	281	312	342
9	9	40	68	99	129	160	190	221	252	282	313	343
10	10	41	69	100	130	161	191	222	253	283	314	344
11	11	42	70	101	131	162	192	223	254	284	315	345
12	12	43	71	102	132	163	193	224	255	285	316	346
13	13	44	72	103	133	164	194	225	256	286	317	347
14	14	45	73	104	134	165	195	226	257	287	318	348
15	15	46	74	105	135	166	196	227	258	288	319	349
16	16	47	75	106	136	167	197	228	259	289	320	350

17	17	48	76	107	137	168	198	229	260	290	321	351
18	18	49	77	108	138	169	199	230	261	291	322	352
19	19	50	78	109	139	170	200	231	262	292	323	353
20	20	51	79	110	140	171	201	232	263	293	324	354
21	21	52	80	111	141	172	202	233	264	294	325	355
22	22	53	81	112	142	173	203	234	265	295	326	356
23	23	54	82	113	143	174	204	235	266	296	327	357
24	24	55	83	114	144	175	205	236	267	297	328	358
25	25	56	84	115	145	176	206	237	268	298	329	359
26	26	57	85	116	146	177	207	238	269	299	330	360
27	27	58	86	117	147	178	208	239	270	300	331	361
28	28	59	87	118	148	179	209	240	271	301	332	362
29	29		88	119	149	180	210	241	272	302	333	363
30	30		89	120	150	181	211	242	273	303	334	364
31	31		90		151		212	243		304		365

Note: For leap years, the number of any day after February 28 is one plus the tabular number shown.

APPENDIX 2: STATE REAL ESTATE TRANSFER TAXES

The following table presents information gathered by the Federation of Tax Administrators regarding state taxes levied on the sale or transfer of real property located in each state. Included in the chart are a description of the tax, the tax rate expressed as a percentage, and the amount of state revenues collected from state transfer taxes in 2004, expressed in dollars and as a per capita amount.

Key Findings of the FTA include:

- Thirty-five states plus D.C. impose a tax on the transfer of real property located in the state.

- Tax rates range from a low of 0.01% in Colorado to a high of 2.2% in D.C.

- In seven states and D.C., the state tax rate is 1.0% or greater.

- In about $^2/_3$ of the states imposing the tax, the rate is below 0.5% of the value of the transfer.

- In California, Louisiana, and Ohio, real estate transfer taxes are imposed only at the local level.

- Some localities in Delaware, Maryland, Michigan, New Jersey, Pennsylvania, Washington, and West Virginia may impose a tax in addition to the state transfer tax.

Real estate transfer taxes (sometimes called deed recordation taxes) are imposed on the sale or transfer of real property located in the state. The tax is usually based on or measured by the consideration paid for or the fair market value of the real estate. The local official responsible for recording deeds to real estate commonly collects the tax, and it must be paid prior to the deed to the property being recorded. In a number of instances, the tax is paid and evidenced by the affixing of stamps to the deed. There is often a link between the real estate transfer tax and property tax administration. Information gathered in administering the real estate transfer tax is frequently used to ascertain the fair market value of parcels of property to assist in property appraisals and in conducting sales-assessment ratio studies.

In fiscal year 2004, real estate transfer taxes produced about $7 billion in state tax revenue, according to Census Bureau figures. In 15 states, the state transfer tax yielded less than $20 per capita in 2004. The yield at the state level, however, exceeded $100 per capita in Connecticut, Florida, New Hampshire, and Washington State, as well as the District of Columbia where the 2.2% rate generated nearly $500 per capita in 2004. The revenue yield is obviously determined by the tax rate, relative real estate prices, and in the case of D.C., the role of the commercial real estate market relative to the city as a whole.

The table presents state tax revenues as presented by the Bureau of the Census. Where a portion of the revenues is retained by local governments or where there are local transfer taxes, those revenues are not reflected here. Several states indicated their actual revenues differed somewhat from those reported by the Census Bureau. In the interest of consistency, Census Bureau figures were used. The figure reported by Census for Florida was reduced by 40% (as recommended by Florida) to reflect other stamp and document recordation taxes included in Census Bureau totals.

State Real Estate Transfer/Deed Recordation Taxes

State	Description	Rate in Percent	2004 State Revenue ($000)	2004 State Revenue Per Capita
Alabama	$.50 per $500 of property conveyed	0.10%	$45,080	$9.95
Arizona	$2 per deed required to be recorded	N/A	N/A	N/A
Arkansas	$3.30 per $1,000 of consideration in excess of $100	0.33%	$25,972	$9.43
California	Local taxes only		N/A	N/A
Colorado	$.01 per $100 of consideration in excess of $500	0.01%	N/A	N/A
Connecticut	1.25% of consideration paid if consideration exceeds $2,000; other rates for commercial transfers	1.25%	$175,816	$50.18

State	Description	Rate in Percent	2004 State Revenue ($000)	2004 State Revenue Per Capita
Delaware	2 to 3% (depending on local tax) on transfers in excess of $100; 1% on contracts for improvements to realty in excess of $10,000	2.0 – 3.0%	$98,566	$118.74
D.C.	2.2% of consideration or fair market value	2.20%	$286,269	$485.20
Florida	$.70 per $100 of consideration, except in Miami-Dade County where it is $.60 per $100	0.70%	$1,950,402	$111.99*
Georgia	$1 for first $1,000 of consideration, plus $.10 per $100 of additional consideration	0.10%	$420	$0.05
Hawaii	$.10 per $100 of consideration	0.10%	$18,426	$14.59
Illinois	$.50 per each $500 of value or fraction of $50	0.10%	N/A	N/A
Iowa	$.80 per $500 paid for the real property transferred	0.16%	$13,869	$4.69
Kansas	0.26% of debt or obligation secured by real estate	0.26%	$52,569	$14.59
Kentucky	$.50 per $500 of value conveyed in deed	0.10%	$3,434	$0.83
Louisiana	Local taxes only			
Maine	$2.20 per $500 of value conveyed – split between grantor and grantee	0.44%	$29,380	$22.31

State	Description	Rate in Percent	2004 State Revenue ($000)	2004 State Revenue Per Capita
Maryland	0.5 percent of consideration paid for realty – also local deed recordation taxes ranging from $2.20 to $5.00 per $500 of value and local transfer taxes ranging up to 1.5% of consideration paid	Variable depending on local rates	$183,189	$32.96
Massachusetts	$4.56 per $1,000 of consideration	0.46%	$245,906	$38.32
Michigan	$3.75 per $500 of value for property being transferred plus local taxes of $.55 to $.75 per $500 of value	0.75%	$317,480	$31.39
Minnesota	$1.65 plus .33% of value in excess of $500 plus .23% of debt secured by real estate for mortgage registry	0.56%	$352,354	$69.08
Nebraska	$2.25 per $1,000 of value transferred	0.23%	$9,215	$5.27
Nevada	$1.95 to $2.55 per $500 of consideration depending on population of county	0.255% max.	$96,704	$41.41
New Hampshire	$1.50 per $100 of consideration split equally between buyer and seller	1.50%	$145,386	$111.82

State	Description	Rate in Percent	2004 State Revenue ($000)	2004 State Revenue Per Capita
New Jersey	Four transfer fees – Basic is $1.25 state and $.50 county each $500 of consideration; additional fees range from $.25 to $4.30 per $500 of consideration; a fifth fee of 1% is imposed on buyers for an entire consideration in excess of $1 million for certain residential and farmland property	1.21% max. if less than $1 million	$246,503	$28.34
New York	$2.00 per $500 of consideration. An additional 1% on transfers of a personal residence of more than $1 million	0.4% on the basic tax, plus an additional 1.0% on residences over $1 million	$510,443	$26.55
North Carolina	$1 per $500 of consideration or value transferred with 51% of revenue retained at local level	0.20%	$54,940	$6.43
Ohio	Local taxes only ranging from $.10 to $.40 per $100 of value	0.4% max.		
Oklahoma	$.75 per $500 of consideration	0.15%	$12,048	$3.42
Pennsylvania	1% of consideration or fair market value with local transfer taxes of 1 to 3%	4.0% max.	$470,789	$37.95
Rhode Island	$2 per $500 of consideration	0.40%	$12,645	$11.70

State	Description	Rate in Percent	2004 State Revenue ($000)	2004 State Revenue Per Capita
South Carolina	$1.85 per $500 of value with $.55 per $500 retained at the local level	0.37%	$50,493	$12.03
South Dakota	$.50 per $500 of consideration payable by grantor	0.10%	$141	$0.18
Tennessee	$.37 per $100 of consideration, plus a mortgage tax of $.115 per $100 of indebtedness in excess of $2,000	0.49%	$174,206	$29.52
Vermont	1.25% of value of property transferred; lower rates on certain homes and farms	1.25% max.	$20,762	$33.43
Virginia	$.25 per $100 of conveyance, plus $.50 per $500 of consideration for transfer of realty	0.35%	$340,591	$45.66
Washington	1.28% of selling price, plus local tax of 0.3 to 0.5%	1.33% max.	$640,086	$103.17
West Virginia	$1.10 per $500 of consideration, plus local taxes that may run to another $1.10 per $500	0.44% max.	$10,129	$5.58
Wisconsin	$.30 per $100 of value	0.30%	$66,325	$12.04
U.S. Total			$6,615,458	25.33**

* Revenue figures adjusted to eliminate taxes other than real estate transfers in the Census Bureau figures.

** U.S. Median

Source: FTA compilation based on CCH, State Tax Handbook (2006), data from the U.S. Bureau of the Census, Governments Division, and information from individual states.

APPENDIX 3: RESIDENTIAL PROPERTY TAX RATES FOR THE LARGEST CITY IN EACH STATE 2004

The real property tax is a function of housing values, real estate tax rates, assessment levels, homeowner exemptions, and credits. The effective rate is the amount each jurisdiction considers based on the assessment level used. The assessment level is a ratio of assessed value to assumed market value. Nominal rates represent the "announced" rates levied by the jurisdiction.

City	Effective tax rate per $100 Rank	Assessment Rate	Nominal Level (percent)	Rate /$100
Houston, TX	1	2.99	100.0	2.99
Providence, RI	2	2.97	100.0	2.97
Indianapolis, IN	3	2.78	100.0	2.78
Bridgeport, CT	4	2.73	70.0	3.90
Philadelphia, PA	5	2.64	32.0	8.26
Manchester, NH	6	2.64	100.0	2.64
Milwaukee, WI	7	2.54	96.8	2.63
Baltimore, MD	8	2.46	100.0	2.46
Newark, NJ	9	2.30	94.7	2.43
Des Moines, IA	10	2.21	48.5	4.56
Portland, ME	11	2.20	82.0	2.68
Omaha, NE	12	2.08	94.0	2.21
Jacksonville, FL	13	1.98	98.0	2.02
Fargo, ND	14	1.89	3.9	48.41
Detroit, MI	15	1.86	27.8	6.71
Columbia, SC	16	1.84	4.0	46.10
Chicago, IL	17	1.74	22.1	7.88
New Orleans, LA	18	1.74	10.0	17.40
Memphis, TN	19	1.73	23.8	7.27
Boise, ID	20	1.73	97.3	1.78
Atlanta, GA	21	1.72	40.0	4.29
Jackson, MS	22	1.71	10.0	17.09

Anchorage, AK	23	1.63	100.0	1.63
Sioux Falls, SD	24	1.56	85.0	1.84
Billings, MT	25	1.55	80.0	1.94
Burlington, VT	26	1.54	67.6	2.28
Salt Lake City, UT	27	1.51	99.0	1.53
Columbus, OH	28	1.49	30.3	4.91
Portland, OR	29	1.43	64.2	2.23
Wilmington, DE	30	1.39	51.2	2.71
Little Rock, AR	31	1.38	20.0	6.90
Phoenix, AZ	32	1.32	10.0	13.21
Wichita, KS	33	1.31	11.5	11.43
Minneapolis, MN	34	1.31	88.6	1.48
Albuquerque, NM	35	1.27	33.3	3.80
Los Angeles, CA	36	1.25	100.0	1.25
Boston, MA	37	1.23	100.0	1.23
Oklahoma City, OK	38	1.20	11.0	10.91
Kansas City, MO	39	1.20	19.0	6.30
New York City, NY	40	1.16	8.0	14.46
Charlotte, NC	41	1.13	95.8	1.18
Louisville, KY	42	1.10	90.0	1.23
Las Vegas, NV	43	1.09	35.0	3.12
Virginia Beach, VA	44	1.08	88.7	1.22
Seattle, WA	45	1.03	94.1	1.09
Washington, D.C.	46	0.96	100.0	0.96
Charleston, SC	47	0.88	60.0	1.47
Birmingham, AL	48	0.70	10.0	6.95
Cheyenne, WY	49	0.68	9.5	7.11
Denver, CO	50	0.53	8.0	6.69
Honolulu, HI	51	0.38	100.0	0.38
Unweighted Average	(X)	1.62	59.3	6.29
Median	(X)	1.54	(X)	(X)
SYMBOL X implies not applicable				

Source: Government of the District of Columbia, Office of the Chief Financial Officer, Tax Rates and Revenues, Tax Burden Comparisons, Nationwide Comparison, 2004. http://cfo. dc.gov/cfo/frames.asp?doc=/cfo/lib/cfo/services/studies/City04STUDY.pdf\

APPENDIX 5: INVESTMENT AND REAL ESTATE FORMULAS AT A GLANCE

1	Present Value = Cash flow	$PV =$ $N =$ $i =$	$FV \div (1 + i)^N$ $\log (FV/PV) \div \log (1 + i)$ $(FV/ PV)^{1/N} - 1$
2	Simple Interest	$I =$ $S =$ $S =$ $P =$	Prt $P + I$ $P(1 + rt)$ $S \div (1 + rt)$ where: P = principal, expressed in dollars r = annual rate, expressed as a percent t = term, expressed in years or a fractional part of a year I = total interest, expressed in dollars S = amount or sum of the principal and interest, expressed in dollars Exact interest, which is based on 365-day year is always less than ordinary and banker's interest, which are based on a 360-day year.
3	Simple Discount		Present value – value at maturity Simple interest on P = discount on S
4	Interest Bearing Debts		Step 1: Determine the date of maturity for the note. Step 2: Compute the value of the debt at maturity. P(1 + rt) to determine value of debt at maturity, using the rate of a note. Step 3: Determine the discount period. $S \div (1 + rt)$ to determine the PV of the debt at maturity, using the rate money is worth. Step 4: Compute the proceeds (or sum received).

5	Interest Bearing Debts	$D =$	Sdt
		$P_b =$	$S - D$
		$P_b =$	$S(1 - dt)$
		$S =$	$P_b \div (1 - dt)$
			where:
			S = maturity value of the note
			t = number of years, or fractional part of a year, between the date of discount and the maturity date of the note
			d = the annual bank discount
			D = the bank discount
			P_b = bank proceeds
6	Compound Interest (regular periods of conversion)	$S =$	$P(1 + i)^n$
		$P =$	$S \div (1 + i)^n$
		$n =$	$(\log S - \log P) \div \log(1 + i)$
			where:
			P = principal or present value
			i = interest rate per period
			n = number of interest periods
			S = compound amount or sum of the principal and interest
			m = frequency of conversion (per year)
			j = nominal interest rate
			$j \div m$
		$i =$	$t * m$
		$n =$	
			nominal rate = annual rate
			periodic rate = rate per period
			periodic rate = $(1 + i)^n - 1$
			effective rate = rate of increase
7	Compound Discount		The compound interest on P in n periods =
			The discount on S at compound interest

8	Depreciation	$R =$	$(C - S) \div n$
		$R =$	$B \div n$
			Where: C = original cost S = salvage value n = estimated life (in years) R = annual depreciation expense B = base value to reproduce or replace
9	Breakeven Point for Paying Points	Break-even =	cost of points $\div$ monthly savings
10	Annuity	$S_n =$	$R * \dfrac{(1 + i)^n - 1}{i}$
		$S_n =$	$R * s_{n|i}$
		$A_n =$	$R * \dfrac{1 - (1 + i)^n}{i}$
		$A_n =$	$Ra_{n|t}$
		$R =$	$A_n * \dfrac{i}{a_{n|i}}$
		$S_{n|i} =$	$S_n \div R$ where: n = the number of periods R = periodic rent or the amount of each payment i = rate of interest per period S_n = the amount of an annuity; the sum of the accumulated payments at a given period in time (also called the accumulated amount of an annuity) Term = the length of time for which payments are to continue as measured from the beginning of the first period to the end of the last period Interval = interval between payments
11	Amortization	$A_n =$	$R * a_{n|i}$
		$R =$	$A_n * \dfrac{1}{a_{n|i}}$

12	Sinking Fund Amortization	R=	$S_n * \dfrac{i}{s_{n\|i}}$ where: n = the number of periods R = periodic rent or the amount of each payment i = rate of interest per period S_n = the sum of the accumulated payments at a given period in time
13	Bond Yield	V=	$F(1 + i)^{-n} + R *a_{n\|i}$ where: F = the face value of the bond V= the value of the bond at the desired yield to maturity R = the amount of each periodic interest payment; If the bond is a coupon bond, then R = F*r i = the yield rate per period on the present value n = the number of interest periods to maturity; if the bond is a coupon bond, then n is the number of coupons still attached to the bond
14	Bond Perpetuities	PV= (perpetuity) Periodic Income = Value =	$R \div 1$ where: i = yield R = periodic payment yield * value periodic income $\div$ yield
15	Bond Capitalized Costs	K = K =	$C + [(S \div i)* (1 \div S\, a_{k\|i})]$ $(S \div i)* (1 \div S\, a_{k\|i})$ if assets must be replaced in their entirety where: i = rate of interest per period S = the amount of an annuity; the sum of the accumulated payments at a given period in time k = number of periods c = original cost

16	IRS Depreciation	Annual Depreciation =	depreciable basis ÷ number of allowable years
17	Straight Line Depreciation	$R=$ $R=$	$(C - S) \div n$ $B \div n$ where: C = original cost S = salvage value n = estimated life (in years) R = the annual depreciation expense B = base cost to reproduce or replace
18	Sinking Fund Depreciation	$R =$ $BV_k =$ $C=$	$(C - S) * \dfrac{1}{s_{n\|i}}$ $C - R * s_{k\|i}$ $BV_k + (R * s_{k\|i})$ where: S = salvage value n = estimated life (in years) C = cost of an asset BV_k = book value at period k $s_{n\|i}$ = value from the annuity table, given n years at rate i $s_{k\|i}$ = value from the annuity table, given k periods at rate i
19	Constant Percentage or Declining Balance Depreciation	$BV_k =$ $S =$ $C =$	$C(1 - r)^k$ $C(1 - r)^n$ $S \div (1 - r)^n$ where: S = salvage value > 0 C = cost of an asset BV_k = book value and the book value at the end of k years $BV_k = C * r$ at the end of the first year
20	Net Present Value	$NPV=$	PV – investment amount
21	Profitability Index	=	Present value of all future cash flows ÷ initial cash investment

22	Present Value of Income Stream	PV =	= income ÷ cap rate
23	Gross Scheduled income	=	Annual rent from income properties
24	Gross Operating Income	GOI =	gross scheduled income – vacancy allowance – credit loss
25	Net Operating Income	NOI =	gross scheduled income – operating expenses – vacancy allowance
26	Debt Service Coverage Ratio	DSCR =	NOI ÷ (principle + interest)
27	Weighted Average Cost of Capital	WACC =	$(B ÷ B + S) * R_B + (S ÷ B + S) * R_s$ where: B = the value of bonds or debt S = the value of stocks or equity R = the cost of debt or interest rate of debt R = the cost of equity or the expected return on equity
28	Net Income Return on Investment	Net Income ROI =	(gross income – operating expenses – interest – depreciation) ÷ owner's equity
29	Cash Return on Investment	Cash ROI =	remaining cash after debt service ÷ cash investment
30	Total Return on Investment	Total ROI =	(remaining cash after debt service + principal reduction) ÷ cash investment
31	Return on Equity	ROE =	cash flow after taxes ÷ initial cash investment Or cash flow after taxes ÷ (resale value – mortgage balance)

32	Capitalization Rate	Cap Rate =	NOI ÷ sales price
33	Sale Price	=	NOI ÷ cap rate
34	Operating Efficiency Ratio	OER =	Total operating expenses ÷ square feet
35	Gross Rent Multiplier	GRM =	Purchase price ÷ gross scheduled income
36	Operating Ratio	OR =	Operating expenses ÷ gross income
37	Break Even Ratio	BER =	total operating expense + debt service ÷ gross income
38	Housing Expense Ratio	=	PITI ÷ monthly gross income
39	Total Obligations Ratio	=	PITIO – other long term debts ÷ monthly gross income
40	Loan to Value Ratio	LTV =	Loan amount ÷ purchase price or appraised value
41	Spread of Leverage	=	ROA – Cost of Funds Must be positive, otherwise the investment offers a negative return
42	IRS Depreciation Allowance	=	$$\frac{\text{Total purchase price} - \text{value of land}}{\text{number of allowable years}}$$

REFERENCES

Berges, S. (2004) *The Complete Guide to Real Estate Finance for Investment Properties- How to Analyze Single-Family, Multi-Family or Commercial Property*, John Wiley & Sons Inc.

Crawford, L.L. (2005) *Gaines and Coleman Real Estate Math- What You Need to Know*, 6th Ed, Dearborn Real Estate Education.

Gaines, G. Jr.; Coleman, D.S.; Crawford, L.L. (1996) *Real Estate Math- Explanations, Problems, Solutions*, 5th Ed, Dearborn Real Estate Education.

Gallinelli, F. (2004) *What Every Real Estate Investor Needs to Know About Cash Flow... and 36 Other Key Financial Measures*, McGraw-Hill.

Tamper, R. (2002) *Mastering Real Estate Math*, 7th Edition, Dearborn Real Estate Education.

AUTHOR DEDICATION & BIOGRAPHY

This book is dedicated to the defunct proverbial village of Walbrook Junction, Baltimore. Many thanks to Arnett, Bou, Spanky, Mark, Snoot, and Woods.

Inspired by the rich culture of inner city life, Jamaine Burrell prides herself on being capable to combine all acquired talents to produce a result. She holds a BS in mathematics from Coppin State University-Baltimore. She held the position of Army Operations Research Analyst for more than sixteen years, and she writes freelance for the sport of writing. Jamaine has authored several other books under Atlantic Publishing.

INDEX